Multicultural Picture Books:
Art for Understanding Others

By Sylvia and Kenneth Marantz

A Publication of THE BOOK REPORT & LIBRARY TALK
Professional Growth Series

Linworth Publishing, Inc.
Worthington, Ohio

Library of Congress Cataloging-in-Publication Data

Marantz, Sylvia S.
    Multicultural picture books : art for understanding others / by
Sylvia and Kenneth Marantz.
        p.   cm. -- (Professional growth series)
    "A publication of The book report & Library talk."
    Includes bibliographical references.
    ISBN 0-938865-22-6.
    1. Children--United States--Books and reading. 2. Children's
literature, English--Bibliography. 3. Picture books for children-
-United States--Bibliography. 4. Minorities--United States-
-Juvenile literature--Bibliography. I. Marantz, Kenneth A.
II. Title. III. Series.
Z1037.M267   1994
[PR990]
016.62--dc20

93-50811
                                                                          CIP

Published by Linworth Publishing, Inc.
480 East Wilson Bridge Road, Suite L
Worthington, Ohio   43085

Copyright © 1994 by Linworth Publishing, Inc.

Series Information:

From The Professional Growth Series

ISBN 0-938865-22-6

5 4 3 2

Table of Contents

Introduction

Who are Kenneth and Sylvia Marantz and why have they entered the arena of multiculturalism, cultural pluralism, and political correctness? We are, respectively, a professor of art education and art educator for some 40 years and a teacher-librarian who has worked with books and young people for as long or longer. About art and books we speak with some authority. We are also both first-generation Americans who have lived the experience of the outsider and the pain of prejudice. Beyond this, we have travelled extensively over the years throughout the world, hosted by colleagues and ex-students who have shared their lands and cultures with us.

But we are not anthropologists. Certainly many others know much more than we do about both individual cultures and the subject of multicultural education. We realize that however hard we try, we cannot be value-neutral, because language itself is not value-neutral. Everyone can find something offensive in what seems innocuous to others. What we are doing here, after reading all the references we could find and consulting with members of many ethnic and cultural groups, is trying our best to bring to the attention of librarians and teachers some examples of what we think are quality picture books about many cultures, illustrated with art that reflects aspects of the culture concerned.

Our continuing concern for the appreciation of the art of the picture book is really why we have stepped into the arena. Over the years, many fine picture books have, we feel, reflected with respect the art of the country or group about which the story is told. This makes these books ideal for helping children understand and appreciate the art and culture of others. It also gives respect and a sense of identity to children from the culture represented. So we present here a selection, mainly from the last five years but including some outstanding older examples still in print, of books we feel will help attain these goals.

How did we make our selection? We have been collecting picture books with a project like this in mind for the past several years. We have followed up reviews and references, using a large public library. Obviously this selection is not exhaustive or complete, but we feel it is a good beginning. Our first criterion is a good story, one that holds the interest of children but also is culture-specific, including at least some quality of the spiritual life of that culture. Next, the illustrations should display artistic competence; the artist's people should look believable, the handling of media should show some skill. Primarily the qualities of the style of that cultural group, either historic or contemporary, should be reflected in the art. If the art style is "translated" for Western eyes, the cultural sensibilities should still be apparent, for example, the unity of man and nature in the culture of Native Americans. Finally, the text and the pictures should work together, as in any successful picture book, to make an entity.

How are the selected books arranged? We have arbitrarily divided the world into areas. Readers will note that the section on Europe is truncated; the reasons for this are discussed in the introduction to that section. First in each section are listed books of original tales or folk tales that reflect the past. Then come picture books about more contemporary life in these areas. Finally, where available, come books about the experiences of immigrants from these areas to the United States. Some related informational and background books are listed. Although there is a great deal available, we have not included audiovisual materials. For those who wish to further pursue information, the bibliography offers many sources upon which to draw.

We hope this book is only a beginning, a spur to further exploration of the ever-growing number of picture books from many cultures.

Kenneth and Sylvia Marantz

Section 1

Why Should Children Become Involved with Picture Books Depicting Many Cultures?

The world beyond their family and neighborhood becomes part of children's lives when they are very young. Television images of other places and peoples pass in front of their eyes. From small towns in the Midwest to large cities and their suburbs, populations now reflect more people from different cultural backgrounds than ever before in U.S. history.

As Robert C. Branch and Michelle R. Rice in "Cultural Sensitivity in Media Selection" (*Ohio Media Spectrum*, Spring 1992, p. 25) define it, "Culture is recognized as the feelings, the patterns of thinking, and the actions of human groups, including traditional ideas and their attached values." Although other countries experience the clash of new cultures upon established mores, the United States and Canada have traditionally been the scene of the most obvious attempts at assimilation, of "melting pots," of making a new culture from those of the many new arrivals. In recent years the U.S. education system has tried to be, by necessity, multicultural.

As noted in the Introduction, the controversy over multiculturalism in schools cannot be ignored when making the selection of picture books for this book. It is necessary to go beyond the arguments over whose culture should be studied, by whom, and to what extent, to keep in mind the goals of multicultural education that most can agree are beneficial: enhancing the self-esteem of children of all cultures and the respect for the culture of others, while expanding their aesthetic as well as their cultural horizons.

It may be helpful to understand some of the thinking that has shaped the efforts of educators to select materials for multicultural education. As defined in the *Encyclopedia of Educational Research* (Macmillan 1992, v.3, p.870), multicultural education is "a process whose major aim is to change the social structure and culture of schools and other educational institutions so that students from all cultural, racial, ethnic, gender, and social-class groups will have an equal opportunity to experience academic success." This is much more than the simple goal of assimilating new groups of immigrants into the mainstream, which was the prevalent one until after the Second World War.

Intergroup or intercultural education, or ethnic studies, first rose in this period to reduce the tensions that seemed to be growing between races in this country. The civil rights movement of the 1960s spurred the implementation of such studies, and much of the literature on the subject dates from the 1970s. But as the tensions became less evident, the attention to the subject in academic circles dropped. In the past few years, however, the interest in multiculturalism in education has risen sharply. One reason has been a resurgence in demand for minority recognition. Another has been the arrival in the United States of an unusually large influx of immigrants, some refugees from war or oppression, some merely seeking a better life for themselves and their children.

As an example of the increase in attention to this concern, the February 1992 issue of *Wilson Library Bulletin* was devoted to "Librarians: Meeting the Ethnic Challenge." In an article titled "Mainstreaming Library Services to Multicultural Populations: the Evolving Tapestry" (p. 28), Shelley Quesada describes the "rapidly changing ethnic and racial composition of the United States. Initial results from the 1990 census now confirm the reality experienced by those working in social service agencies, libraries, schools, and adult learning centers across the country: the face of America is changing, and changing rapidly.... In many communities throughout the United States the term 'ethnic and racial minorities' is being replaced by the term 'emerging majorities'." We must learn to get along with each other.

More specifically, several aims emerge from the ever-growing current literature on multicultural education. The first is concerned with the children of the minority cultures themselves, and their special needs. Such children face many well-documented hurdles as they try to become successful citizens, among which may be the learning of a new language along with the understanding of an alien culture. For their self-esteem, these children need to feel that their own culture is recognized in their classrooms as valid; they should see role models from their own background with whom they can identify. The need for pride and self-respect is a concern stated in most of the current writing. For example, Branch and Rice assert in their discussion of cultural sensitivity that "When values that have been taught at home conflict with what is presented in the classroom, learners risk being adversely affected. The dilemma of opposing values tends to impact the learner's self-esteem, a major variable in the learning process."

Multicultural education is also concerned with the task of offering a global perspective for all children, who will be living in both a multicultural society and an ever-encroaching multicultural world. "By helping children and families develop an appreciation for all cultures and backgrounds while retaining their own customs and ethnic identity, some progress toward harmony can be made," says *Cultural Awareness for Children* (Addison-Wesley, 1992, p. ix) in a discussion of the program at the Learning Tree School in Dallas, Texas. Other aims cited in current multicultural education writing include the achievement of social cohesion with cultural diversity, an almost impossible balance to maintain. Indeed, in *Multicultural Education; Principles and Practices* (Routledge and Kegan Paul, 1986), James Lynch says that many of his colleagues consider multicultural education to be "a placebo for the continued injustice and inequality in education and society." But he sees the "need for a composite, holistic, multidisciplinary, sequenced and continuous approach to the development of a multicultural curriculum," which will offer the possibility of meeting the needs of the minorities along with the need to live together in harmony.

In addition to the books and periodical articles available to help educators in their multicultural tasks, at least two periodicals are entirely devoted to this subject. In the Fall 1992 issue of *Teaching Tolerance*, James A. Banks, internationally known scholar and director of the Center for Multicultural Education at the University of Washington, defines multicultural education and how it should work to ease racial tensions in light of the Los Angeles riot of 1992.

In another relevant periodical, *Multicultural Review*, Brenda Mitchell-Powell writes in her April 1992 editorial: "After all, appreciation of our common culture and values is enhanced by a recognition of the multiplicity of contributions. Ignorance of differing cultures and human valuation based on economics or class merely reinforce and perpetuate stereotypes ... educational systems in pluralistic societies should offer a framework for learning that enables and encourages students—and teachers—to think and to make informed, experientially based assumptions ... we must cultivate attitudes and environments that recognize society's distinct groups as inseparable from the whole. We owe children the benefit of every opportunity to explore and understand the world and its peoples. Ultimately, when we empower our children, we empower ourselves."

This possibility of empowerment is one reason multicultural education is not universally supported. *Empowerment Through Multicultural Education*, edited by Christine E. Sleeter, (SUNY Press, 1991) includes articles about the effects of such education. Valerie Ooka Pang in "Teaching Children About Social Issues: Kidpower" describes some activities teachers can use, concluding: "Multicultural education moves to empower even our youngest citizens to think about issues in their world and to challenge those arenas of life that they find unjust," an exciting concept, but one which may make some people nervous.

Another source of continual controversy in discussion of multiculturalism is the fear that "traditional Western values" will be lost, or that the curriculum will no longer include the so-called "canon" of knowledge. This has been countered by claims that such traditions are those of the power structure of white, Anglo-Saxon, Protestant males. These continuing arguments should be kept in mind when examining and when using this selection of multicultural picture books with children.

<u>Notes</u>

Section 2
How Do We Define and Evaluate a Multicultural Picture Book?

The field of children's literature is replete with attempts to define picture books, all of which have some merit. For the purposes of this book, we will consider the picture book as one that tells a story either in pictures alone or in almost equal partnership with some text. How many words are too many to create an unbalanced partnership? Only our instinctive response to a specific book permits an answer. Our approach, therefore, places candidates somewhere on a continuum from the totally textless work to those with only a handful of illustrations. The potency of the pictures in contributing to the story rather than the number of pictures per page becomes the test.

Our concerns center around the means by which the visual qualities of picture books affect their abilities to tell stories about people who may hold values and practice behaviors different from those of the readers. Part of our analyses deals with the informational content and part with the feelings generated about that information, what is often referred to as the "emotional content." In their efforts to convey aspects of an existing society, picture books have been labeled with words like factual, genuine, real, honest, true, verifiable, accurate, authoritative, or the really difficult, "authentic." Perhaps there are so many different words to refer to an essentially common notion because of the significance of this concept or idea in our lives. Certainly, it is difficult to come up with a working definition of the "authentic" because human society is not some neat theoretical abstraction but rather a very messy mixture.

Culture refers to the way people behave in specific circumstances, what they value and believe. What can we do to describe, with "authenticity," a culture? If we give it a name, i.e., Jewish or African American, does that mean it really exists as such? In what ways can we provide a "genuine" picture of American culture? Are there values, beliefs, behaviors that all of us have in common? If the American population is too large for that, then how many people make a culture that we can make "true" statements about, statements that can be supported by others, or by "facts?" And who are the others who provide the facts?

Although the notion of culture is so tenuous, it has been used for political purposes, for example, the Nazi claim of Aryan superiority or current Serbian actions toward "ethnic cleansing." On the positive side, there is a need to help specific groups of Americans achieve a greater feeling of self, an identification with the potency of achievements associated with past or present members of their social or ethnic group. The proliferation of books in which strong women star must help young females perceive a future of greater possibilities than their grandmothers could find in the role models of housewife or spinster. The pejorative meaning this last word has acquired has, incidentally, some symbolic visual parallels which we can look for. So the aims of multiculturalism have included emphasizing positive attributes of human societies, the grandeur of Aztec architecture rather than the ritual murders, for example. We will be searching for the means by which artist and designer have approached this aim in picture books.

We must all recognize the impossibility of replicating total cultures "authentically" in a book. The act of bookmaking is a bit like the act of translation; it is an artistic process that involves constant compromise. The success, or "authenticity," of a book depends on the skill of its makers in abstracting a message from the myriad materials available, a message that we, who may be aliens, can understand. The message must also correspond in spirit with the life qualities of the message-makers with whom the book is concerned, that is, some specific cultural group.

In addition, we cannot forget that a picture book is also an art object. The artists/designers have the responsibility to interpret the spirit of the story even if they don't have total freedom of expression. If a story is about a religious rite that involves a traditional object such as a Hanukkah menorah, the shape may be open to variations but it still must have spaces for nine candles. It's okay for Mickey Mouse to have three fingers per hand, but not King Arthur. Mercer Mayer was condemned by some critics for his illustrations for *Everyone Knows What A Dragon Looks Like* (by Jay Williams, Four Winds, 1976) because they were merely a pastiche of Oriental and Western art styles. If he were writing an art history, such criticism would be proper. But did his translation of the spirit of some periods (not all Oriental paintings are the same) of Oriental painting do a disservice or rather did his inventiveness strengthen the message of the narrative? Does a break with "authenticity" invalidate a book, denying its use as a multicultural resource?

The picture book, because it embodies the stories which are the spiritual underpinning of any group of people, has great potential for bridging the differences among us. The concept of story is one common to all of us, a shared experience that sets the stage for communication. Most young children have been introduced to the myths and fables that are part of their culture. So picture books based on similar if alien legends, as well as those based on daily life, have a decent chance of being absorbed. But what can be learned depends on the insights and craftsmanship of those producing the objects we study. And we can only do our best in assessing these for you.

We are suggesting that picture books can at least help children get a flavor of another way of perceiving life. That means that we adults working with the children and books must in some cases not only help them understand the meaning of the words of a story but also seek ways to "translate" the pictures. We admit our ambivalence concerning the possibility of dealing adequately with cross-cultural learning in classrooms. But we believe in the potency of some picture books, which get us involved with issues, concerns, values, and problems common to all humans, but rendered in different ways around the world, or across the city. Those who create these books must understand the people on *both* sides of the bridge they are trying to build. They should try to know what is appropriate for the people concerned. And finally, those who are successful must use their artistic skills to interpret what they want to convey so the reader can be empathetic, can value and be moved by the message. We think the books we have selected succeed in these aims. From these suggestions we hope teachers and librarians can build a curriculum that suits their particular situation while offering as wide a variety of visual experiences from the selected cultures as possible.

By the time this book appears in print, hundreds more picture books will be on the market. Readers who agree with our aim of finding books that have both potency of visual interpretation and the ability to convey a significant message will have to make choices from among these. When doing so, we suggest you ask some of the questions we asked ourselves as we chose the books featured here:

- Does the book tell an appealing story that is also culture-specific?
- Are the illustrations competent? That is., are the representations of objects, humans, and animals, convincingly portrayed? Is there consistency in the use of the media?
- Are the characteristics of the cultural group reflected in some way in the art work?
- Do the text and the pictures complement each other, forming a cohesive unit to "tell" the story?

Notes

Section 3
Asia and the Pacific

Although immigrants from Asia have been coming to the United States through most of our history, they have been missing from most history texts. They have also been, at least until quite recently, a quiet minority not generally protesting the discrimination they have suffered. Like African Americans they can be immediately recognized as members of a minority and are therefore vulnerable to persecution. Japanese Americans have had the added indignities suffered during World War II, including internment in American camps, because Japan was America's enemy.

Changes in immigration laws, obligations following the Vietnam War, and persistent poor economic conditions in some Asian countries have all led to an increase in immigration from this area. As more and more people from Asia become Americans, the need for materials to provide self-esteem for them and to aid understanding and respect from other Americans has grown as well. Considering the rich lode of fantasy and legend in the religion, art, puppet theater, and dance in such cultures as India, Indonesia, and Thailand, it is surprising how little of this is currently reflected in picture books. Publishers are finally giving us some picture books on the lesser-known areas like Sri Lanka; we hope more will be forthcoming.

The cross-currents of cultures and arts along with philosophy and religion over the centuries of civilization in Asia yield certain similarities amid the differences of cultures. Although Japan seems the dominant country now, its culture and art through history have borrowed frequently from its neighbors. Certainly through sheer size alone, China's influences must be recognized. As Buddhism and Hinduism spread they brought certain common themes as well. In examining the selected picture books, we shall see similarities in folk tales and art styles that show this.

Japan and Japanese Americans

Original Tales and Folk Tales Evoking the Past

Keith Baker, **The Magic Fan**. Harcourt Brace, 1989. 32pp.

This original story in folk-tale style incorporates in both words and pictures many elements of life in the Japan of long ago. Yoshi, a young builder, builds what he sees on a magic fan: a boat, a kite, and a bridge. When an earthquake and a *tsunami*, or tidal wave, come, the bridge saves the people of the village. Then Yoshi realizes he does not need the fan to see what needs to be built.

A modulated gray double-page acts as a background for an intensely red, fan-shaped frame that houses the illustrations, with exposed bamboo struts in the center. The small print text on the left side raises a question that is answered in the right-side text. Visually the answer is illustrated by flipping the cut, fan-shaped frame over to disclose another picture, as seen on the "magic-fan." Acrylic paint is applied thinly enough to pick up the texture of the rough-surfaced board on which it is painted. Baker exploits this effect to help model his forms and produce three-dimensional objects and complex scenes of village life. The mixture of stylized reality and a dreamy vision are effectively combined in this imaginative use of the fan-shaped cut-out and frame. The contorted rendition of Namazu the earthquake fish is particularly stunning as it demonstrates the incorporation of traditional decorative forms into a curvilinear space. Grades 1-4.

Ashley Bryan, reteller. **Sh-ko and His Eight Wicked Brothers**. Illustrated by Fumio Yoshimura. Atheneum, 1988. 28pp.

Bryan retells a legendary story that the illustrator, Yoshimura, remembered from his childhood in Japan. In the story, the youngest of nine brothers is teased and tormented by his siblings but wins in the end. When the eight older brothers set out to court a princess in a nearby country, Sh-ko asks to come along and is made to carry the baggage. On the way he meets a skinned rabbit who tells how he lost his fur to crocodiles, but then was further tormented by advice from the wicked brothers. Sh-ko helps the rabbit, receiving in turn a special gift that gains him the princess.

      The illustrations in pale gray ink brushed with rapid strokes on pinkish paper derive directly from a style shown in the 12th-century Japanese scroll called "Frolicking Animals." Solidity is achieved by nuance, slight variations in the thickness and darkness of the lines. Landscapes are more suggested than stated. An example of the potency of restraint to express high adventure and a touch of humor. Grades 1 or 2-4.

Claude Clement, **The Painter and the Wild Swans**. Illustrated by Frederic Clement. Dial, 1986, paper 1990. 26pp.

This story of Teiji, a famous Japanese painter, is an original one inspired by photographs of Siberian swans taken by the Japanese photographer Teiji Saga. One day when Teiji sees beautiful white birds flying by, he can no longer paint, but sets out in quest of them. After surviving cold and hardship, he realizes that painting is not important compared to the natural beauty he has seen. An amazing transformation ends the story, requiring the perspective of an older child for this otherwise simple tale.

      Panels of varying size and in tones of blue on white backgrounds hold both English and Japanese texts. This is a Western interpretation of the misty landscapes seen in Oriental paintings. Swans and water and twisted trees become modulated, and we see physical transformations in sequential panels. Clement's fine example of cinematographic design enhances the magical qualities of this mystical tale. Grades 2 or 3-5 or 6.

Patricia A. Compton, reteller, **The Terrible Eek: A Japanese Tale**. Illustrated by Sheila Hamanaka. Simon & Schuster, 1991. 34pp.

One rainy night, a boy asks his father what he is afraid of. When the father says "a thief," the thief hiding on the roof hears and prepares to steal from them. When he says "among animals, the wolf," a wolf sneaking by hears and also prepares to steal. But when the wolf and the thief hear the father say that what he fears most on a rainy night is "a terrible leak," they do not understand, and think that must be something truly terrible. A slapstick comedy of errors follows, with the thief's fall from the roof onto the wolf, a mad race through the woods, and a gathering of other animals all frightened away by the unknown.

Although oil paints on a textured canvas are not historically used materials in Japan, Hamanaka creates a sense of dramatic contrasts in her paintings that suggest many Japanese stories. From subtly patterned endpapers, solidly painted yellow half-title and title pages through green-blue hued dedication pages, she slyly introduces her three animal characters by having them stick their heads into page corners. Layouts vary from double-page scenes to thin panels, depending on the action. Animals and humans are depicted for strong comic effect rather than anatomical accuracy. The painting is thin with frequent black outlines. Words and pictures complement each other but one wishes for a few more smile-provoking paintings and a few less descriptive paragraphs. For more of Hamanaka's work, see her *Screen of Frogs* and *The Journey* (both Orchard) below. Grades 2-5.

Sheila Hamanaka, **Screen of Frogs: An Old Tale Retold**. Orchard, 1993. 32pp.

Rich but lazy Koji has to sell off his property to buy what he pleases, until he has only his house, a lake, and a mountain left. Dreaming by the mountain, he is approached by a frog, who begs him not to sell the mountain for the sake of the creatures living there. So Koji sells all the furnishings of his house instead, leaving only a blank screen. That night he hears frog noises, sees frog footprints, and finds the screen full of painted frogs. Everyone wants to buy the beautiful screen, but Koji refuses. Instead he seems to acquire some perspective; he begins to work, and soon has a family and a happy life. The night he dies, the frogs disappear from his screen. His family keeps the land, understanding its importance.

Boldly conceived, Hamanaka's illustrations here exploit collage and opaque paint to create double-page spreads able to integrate the simple, large-print text and still maintain an appealing narrative flow. Brush strokes are vigorous, more delicate when defining a striding horse's legs and wildly expressionistic when painting the screen. Costumes, landscapes, objects are all historically Japanese; faces tend to caricature with the goal of the comic story line adapted from a Japanese text, a story that ends with a dreamy, green-y landscape. Grades 1 or 2-4 or 5.

Momoko Ishii, reteller, **The Tongue-Cut Sparrow**. Illustrated by Suekichi Akaba. Translated by Katherine Paterson. Lodestar/Dutton, 1987. 40pp.

A genuine Japanese folk tale is retold originally by a Japanese publisher and "children's book specialist." The translator is an award-winning writer as well. She has kept some Japanese words to add to the flavor. Pronunciation guide and translations are at the end of the story. The tale of a kind man and his greedy wife is one told in other cultures (for example, "The Fisherman and his Wife"). In this version, the wife clips the tongue of the old man's pet sparrow, who flies away. On his way to find the bird and apologize, the old man goes through many hardships. When he finds her, the sparrow rewards him with a box of treasure. His wife wants more, and suffers as a result. The small print, many words, and vocabulary make this a read-aloud or for older readers.

Akaba is a contemporary Japanese artist who uses traditional techniques to give us illustrations reminiscent of some 17th-century prints or the more recent 19th-century comic Japanese work. Black brush strokes on a creamy rice paper create figures, and just enough environmental detail creates mood, without using Western perspective. When the text reads she "headed for the mountains," the pictured scene is of large, lumpy shapes that surround the woman. Touches of color similar to those in Japanese scrolls enhance the emotional effect. Facial exaggerations that tend toward caricature add considerably to the fun. Grades 2-5 or 6.

Ryerson Johnson, **Kenji and the Magic Geese**. Illustrated by Jean and Mou-sien Tseng. Simon & Schuster, 1992. 32pp.

Johnson's original story concerns a young boy from a traditional rice-farming family and their prized painting of flying geese, which must be sold to buy food. Because he believes that the geese in the painting would want to fly with their wild brothers, Kenji ties the painting to a kite for a ride before it is sold, with strange, magical results that enable the family to keep the painting.

The landscape, building, costumes and artifacts suggest a Japan we might know from historic paintings. The sequence of double-page scenes creates an engaging narrative flow that comfortably integrates the relatively brief text into "neutral corners." Line is used to produce characters and details. Watercolors fill in for emotional effects and to produce complete scenes. The illustrations tend to romanticize the bucolic life, to depict only the positive sides, perhaps as the young Kenji might want to perceive them. Grades 1-5.

Eric A. Kimmel, reteller, **The Greatest of All: A Japanese Folktale**. Illustrated by Giora Carmi. Holiday House, 1991. 32pp.

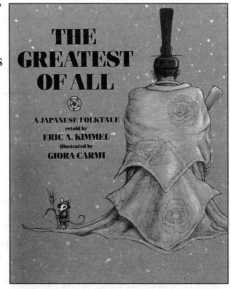

From *The Greatest of All* by Eric A. Kimmel. Illustrated by Giora Carmi. Copyright 1991. Reprinted with permission of Holiday House.

With sly humor, Kimmel recounts the classic tale of the mouse who insists that his daughter cannot marry the humble field mouse of her choice, but only "the greatest of all." His search for the greatest leads to the sun, which the emperor says is greater, to the cloud that hides the sun, to the wind that scatters the clouds, to the wall that blocks the wind, and finally to the field mouse who tunnels within the wall. See Junko Morimoto's *Mouse's Marriage* (Viking) below for a simpler version of the story; also, as mentioned in the author's note on his source, Gerald McDermott's *The Stonecutter* (Viking) below is a variation. A slightly different Chinese version to compare is Carole Kendall's *The Wedding of the Rat Family* (Macmillan).

The thinly bordered illustrations are set on a flecked background suggestive of the fabrics used to mount Oriental paintings. They vary from double-page scenes to vignettes. The text is set in framed cream-color panels. The paintings include bits of architecture and costumes hinting at a historic period. There is a roughness to the style, almost a crude quality to some of the representations of the personified natural phenomena, that seem at odds with our perceptions of Japanese restraint. The page of calligraphed haiku is particularly out of character. Older readers may find it productive to compare these with more traditional illustrations. Grades 1 or 2-5.

Gerald McDermott, **The Stone-cutter: A Japanese Folk Tale**. Viking, 1975; Puffin paper, 1978. 32pp.

In this simply told variation of the tale about rats or mice seeking the mightiest mate, Tasaku, a poor stone-cutter who envies a prince, is turned into a prince by the spirit of the mountains. When he sees the power of the sun, he wants to become the sun. When clouds cover the stone-cutter, he wishes to be a cloud. When the mountain is stronger, he chooses to become a mountain. Then, a lowly stone-cutter begins chipping him away.

The visual narrative depends on abstract symbols derived from Japanese objects. Illustrations are created by cutting shapes from papers previously painted by the artist, e.g., the prince's kimono combines several layers of blue shapes depicting the bulky royal garments, shapes that later appear in black trapped inside the green mountain. Melodramatic in its use of these geometric shapes because the colors are all intense and the scenes are stripped of all but essential details, the pictures contrast with the parts of the white pages that hold the bold. black letters of the text. K-Grade 3 or 4.

Jean Merrill, adapter, **The Girl Who Loved Caterpillars: A Twelfth-Century Tale from Japan**. Illustrated by Floyd Cooper. Philomel, 1992. 32pp.

This unfinished story from an 800-year-old scroll, retold in small print with lengthy text from three English translations, has a feisty, independent heroine. Izumi, the clever, attractive daughter of an official in the emperor's court in Kyoto, is fascinated by insects, worms, toads, and especially caterpillars, an interest no one can understand. Her parents wish she would be more conventional, but she has a mind of her own. Her encounter with a Captain who is curious to see the odd girl he has heard about ends inconclusively; some students might want to write an ending to the story.

Cooper paints portraits, costumes, and settings with opaque pigments in a slightly fuzzy manner to accentuate the romantic qualities of events. Details are few but chosen both to inform and to complement the design of the pages. It is a Westerner observing historical Japan and interpreting its social structure through careful study but in visual ways common to his contemporaries. Cooper paints real people with character; people we can care about as we bridge time and cultures. Grades 2 or 3-6.

Junko Morimoto, **Mouse's Marriage**. Viking, 1986, paper, 1988. 32pp.

This simple retelling of the traditional folk tale is told in more elaborate form in Eric Kimmel's *The Greatest of All* (Holiday House) listed above and in a more elaborate Chinese variation in Carole Kendall's *The Wedding of the Rat Family* (McElderry Books) listed below. Here an elderly mouse couple searching for the best match for their daughter begin by asking the mighty Sun. A cloud covers the Sun before he answers, Wind blows the cloud away, a Wall stops Wind, but tunneling mice crack Wall, making a mouse the best match of all.

Bold delicacy characterizes the full-page pictures, which face the white pages with their brief, large print text. The illustrations are dominated by abstract forms that represent the elements and the Wall. The mice are tiny in the landscapes that contain signs of Japanese culture: the twisted tree, a corner of a tiled roof, a distant pagoda. The text pages also hold thumbnail-size paintings of kites, lanterns, and dolls to add to the sense of place. The final bird's-eye view of the wedding feast is a special light-hearted treat, a scene that summarizes the ability of the artist to marry her cultural sensibilities with a modern mode. K-Grades 3 or 4.

Katherine Paterson, **The Tale of the Mandarin Ducks**. Illustrated by Leo and Diane Dillon. Dutton/Lodestar, 1990. 40pp.

A greedy lord captures and cages a beautiful wild duck in this folk tale retold in a lengthy text by the award-winning author. The duck grieves for his mate, but the lord will not let him go. Yasuko, a kitchen maid, pities and releases the duck, but the steward Shozo is blamed and demoted. The two fall in love. The angry lord wants them put to death, but instead he is ordered to send them to the Imperial Court. On the long journey, they have a strange encounter in the woods, which puts a happy ending to their story.

This is a deliciously designed book from the gold stamped ducks on the red-brown cover to the moody blue-skied forest scene endpapers. It is visually elegant, from the half-title pages with the ducks repeated from the jacket and a few shaggy flowers and the title page's scene of a misty lake shore on through all the pages. Using an 18th-century wood-cut style (ukiyo-e) for illustration, the text is integrated into the two-page spreads, each side designed as one of a pair of prints separated by white borders. Patterns of costumes, flowers, trees, or feathers demonstrate the values placed on such controlled design by this culture. A Caldecott Honor Book. Grades 2-5 or 6.

Helena Clare Pittman, **The Gift of the Willows**. Carolrhoda, 1988. 32pp.

This original story stresses people's relationship with nature as much as the Japanese culture. Yukiyo, a potter, lives happily with his wife Kura by the banks of the Okayama river, where he has watched two willow saplings grow into trees. One summer of drought, he waters and saves them. In the spring, when Kura has just delivered their long-desired child, the river floods. One of the trees falls, making a bridge to safety for the family.

Bits of Japanese life are depicted in the watercolor illustrations: scenes of pottery-making, a koto being played, and a variety of garments worn as the seasons change. A few scenes, like the double-page picture of the bundled-up Yukiyo in a snow storm looking at the willow trees, have emotional impact as the naturalistic representation of human and trees blends with the more impressionistic snow flakes. There's a tendency to break pictorial continuity to no purpose by creating panels separated by the white page, which also breaks the visual narrative flow. Sometimes the painting is heavy-handed or inaccurate in its rendering of a character, again producing puzzling inconsistencies. Grades 2-4.

Robert D. San Souci, **The Samurai's Daughter**. Illustrated by Stephen T. Johnson. Dial, 1992. 32pp.

Based on a legend, this tale of Medieval Japan has a young heroine, Tokoyo, trained by her Samurai father in the warrior's duties as well as those of a lady, and also schooled by the women divers who harvest shellfish. When her father is arrested and exiled by order of a ruler with a disturbed mind, Tokoyo sets out on a difficult journey to join him in exile, becoming his rescuer after battling a sea-serpent.

This is a visual costume drama that emphasizes the large gestures associated with Japanese theatrical performances, moody in the exploitation of colors, e.g. the dappled yellow greens of a forest and the purple reds of a moonlit seascape. Pastel paintings of costumes and boats and bits of architecture suggest a once-upon-a-time Japan. The visual sequence most frequently juxtaposes pages full of text with pages of illustrations of only a part of the narrative, making this a borderline picture book. Notes detail the time setting and the primary sources. Grades 2 or 3-5 or 6.

Dianne Snyder, **The Boy of the Three-Year Nap**. Illustrated by Allen Say. Houghton Mifflin, 1988. 32pp.

In this traditional folk tale from the author's childhood, a lazy but clever boy is the despair of his poor, hard-working mother. Disguised as the *ujigami* or

From *The Gift of the Willows* by Helena Clare Pittman. Copyright 1988. Reprinted with permission of Carolrhoda.

From *The Boy of the Three-Year Nap* by Dianne Snyder. Illustrated by Dianne Snyder. Copyright 1988. Reprinted with permision of Houghton Mifflin.

village god, Taro tricks a wealthy merchant into giving him his daughter in marriage, but is in turn tricked by his mother.

There is a crispness of the black outlines, an evenness of the watercolors that neatly flood them, that call to mind the work of the 19th-century Japanese woodcut masters like Hiroshige. A 20th-century approach to facial and body gestures creates the comic adventures. On the other hand, there are lots of details of a life no longer lived. The scenes are framed in thick black borders and the text appears in the white spaces below. This formal setting doesn't detract from the lively flow of the humorous visual narrative. A Caldecott Honor Book. Grades 2-5.

David Wisniewski, **The Warrior and the Wise Man**. Lothrop, 1989. 32pp.

An original story set in long-ago Japan has a familiar theme: a father sets twin sons a task to prove who should succeed him as emperor. Tozaemon is a brave, fierce warrior, while Toemon is clever but gentle. The test is to bring back the five eternal elements from the demons who guard them. As Tozaemon steals the Earth That Is Ever Bountiful, the Water That Constantly Quenches, the Fire That Burns Forever, the Wind That Always Blows and the Cloud That Eternally Covers, Toemon follows after him, helping to repair the damage his brother has caused in the thefts. When he finally saves the castle, Toemon's wisdom is acknowledged by his father, who appoints him emperor. The story is told simply but with a large amount of text.

The intricacy of cut, solid-color papers that overlap conveys some of the potent visual force found in the scroll paintings that depict the Samurai wars. Costumes, weapons, and decorations are all drawn from 12th-century Japan. Black silhouettes are especially effective in creating scenes that integrate these artifacts and the personified forces of nature. Although the cut-paper medium is not associated with Japanese art history, the thoughtful use of traditional symbols carries a flavor of Japan. The extensive Author's Note describes the time period, the society, the religion, and the arts upon which he has drawn, plus the instances when he has used artistic license, as well as his artistic technique. Grades 2-6.

Sumiko Yagawa, reteller. **The Crane Wife**. Translated from the Japanese by Katherine Paterson. Illustrated by Suekichi Akaba. Morrow, 1981, Mulberry paper. 40pp.

A well-known traditional tale is retold with some Japanese words to add flavor. In this version, a young peasant helps a wounded crane. That night a beautiful woman comes to his door and asks to become his wife. When the need for money arises, she offers to weave cloth for him, but warns him not to look at her while she works. Twice the wonderful cloth she weaves brings a lot of money. The third time, she warns, must be the last. The greed of others persuades the husband to ask her once more, and his curiosity makes him peek at her. The shocking climax and sad end fascinate listeners and readers. A Note to the Reader includes the pronunciation and meaning of the Japanese words.

The somewhat blurred watercolors blend figures with their environment, a style that contains echoes of some traditional Japanese paintings with faces suggested from historical woodcuts. The mood is subdued in keeping with the low key of the story and the eventual sad ending. Restraint and understatement grip more forcefully than blatant melodrama. Grades 2 or 3-5 or 6.

Stories of Japan Today and in Recent History

Terumasa Akio, **Me and Alves: A Japanese Journey**. Illustrated by Yukio Oido. Translated by Susan Matsui. Annick Press, 1993. Paper. 32pp.

A young boy living on a farm on Japan's north island of Hokkaido tells in simple language how a visitor from Brazil comes to stay with his family, despite grandfather's objections. Alves pitches right into helping with the farm work, makes Grandpa happy by listening to his stories, wins the Sumo wrestling tournament at the village festival, talks to the students at school with the other foreign visitors, and is sadly missed when he has to leave. The young narrator is inspired to hope he can visit Alves some day, and also make friends in many countries. The story is based on an actual program to help acquaint the very insular Japanese with outsiders. The author's note explains how the program began.

Beginning with etchings that produce black lines of infinite variety, the artist uses mostly transparent paints to infuse her pictures with emotional content that enhances the narrative flow: marine blues and greens for the ferry scene, reddish tones for the Sumo wrestling match, warm browns for a winter landscape, rich green for a plowed field. The technique also allows for details of everyday objects and events as well as realistic portraits of the many characters. The illustrations occupy two-thirds of each double-spread with the few lines of text printed on a cream-colored background. There is an intimacy of presentation here that unites words and pictures to create the sense of real people and emotions in a part of Japan today. K-Grade 4.

Masako Hidaka, **Girl from the Snow Country**. Translated by Amanda Mayer Stinchecum. Kane/Miller, 1986. 32pp.

Mi-chan lives in the part of northern Japan where the snow piles up in the cold winters. The small girl uses the pointed leaves of the camellia to make ears for the clumps of snow that look like bunnies to her. Bundled against the cold, she walks to market with her mother, stopping to brush the snow from the statue of Jizo, the protector of children. Perhaps he helps her find the perfect berries to make eyes for the snow bunnies she has made. This is one of the few tales of Japan today for younger children.

The endpapers set the stage by depicting in a thin gray watercolor a waterwheel in a mountainous landscape all buried in snow. Color is used mainly for clothing: heavy wrappings that expose only faces. The few details—toys and flowers in the market—are used as much for visual attractiveness as for information. Even Mi-chen's snow rabbits with leafy ears and red berry eyes aren't enough to overcome the weight of all that snow, snow that keeps falling in all scenes. K-Grade 3.

Tetsuya Honda's *Wild Horse Winter* (Chronicle, 1992) makes an interesting companion book about a wild colt who survives a severe winter, based on the actual behavior of the Dosanko horses of Japan in blizzards. Although the setting is Japan, the pictures are not "Japanese" in style. The story is a compelling one, even for younger readers.

Daisaku Ikeda, **The Cherry Tree**. Illustrated by Brian Wildsmith. Translated by Geraldine McCaughrean. Knopf, 1992. 28pp.

In a countryside recovering from war, fatherless Taichi and his sister Yumiko play outside amid the rubble while their mother shines shoes in the nearby town to earn money. One day in autumn they follow a stray cat to a tree that an old man is wrapping in straw. Although the tree hasn't blossomed since the war, he hopes to nurse it back to health. The children help, and hope with him through the long winter. Spring brings blossoms and renewed hope for all. Although the country and war are not specified and the story is simple, parallels can be drawn for older children to post-World-War II Japan.

Wildsmith fills these big pages with details of the abandoned farmhouse with its high thatched roof, of the efforts to bundle and save the old cherry tree, of the birds and animals and people who live in the area. Despite the clothing and some landscape, this is more a universal, mythic vision than one that is specifically Japanese. The same team of writer, illustrator, and translator produced *The Snow Country Prince* (Orchard, 1990), another inspirational story taking place in a northern fishing village in Japan. Grades 2-5 or 6.

Takaaki Nomura, **Grandpa's Town**. Translated by Amanda Mayer Stinchecum. Text in Japanese and English. Kane/Miller, 1991. 32pp.

A young boy who has worried about his grandfather's loneliness spends time with him, stopping at the fish store and the greengrocer's on their way to the public baths. There they meet the grandfather's friends. The boy realizes why his grandfather wants to keep his life in the town instead of moving to live with his family.

Life in a contemporary Japanese town with its shops and public baths is depicted in detailed woodcuts, reminiscent in some ways of the traditional Japanese. Diluted watercolors define the variety of produce at the greengrocer's or the naked bodies of the men in the steamy bath. Both the English and the Japanese text fit comfortably on pages facing the boldly expressive illustrations. Note that at least one librarian was upset by the small "squiggle" of frontal nudity in the bath scenes (see *School Library Journal*, April 1993, p. 86) that is part of the realism. K or Grades 1-4.

Allen Say, **The Bicycle Man**. Houghton Mifflin, 1982, paper 1989. 40pp.

A young boy affectionately remembers his life in school in southern Japan after World War II, in particular one sports day when two American soldiers arrived. One did fantastic tricks on a bicycle and won the prize.

The illustrations depict the people and life he remembers, and are similar in style to those in Say's *How My Parents Learned to Eat* by Ina R. Friedman (Houghton Mifflin) described later.

_____, **Tree of Cranes**. Houghton Mifflin, 1991. 32pp.

Another young boy in Japan celebrates his first Christmas. Into a typical Japanese house his mother brings a touch of the Christmas she remembers from her California childhood. The boy remembers the unusual tree, the present, the snowman, the warmth of family and holiday.

The illustrations are similar to *The Boy of the Three Year Nap* described above in their sense of frozen motion, clean line, Japanese architecture and costume. Each scene is framed with a thin black line, the same line that frames the facing white page with its centered few lines of text. The colors are intense, the characters are realistic, and the details clearly depicted. K-Grade 4.

Fumiko Takeshita, **The Park Bench**. Illustrated by Mamoru Suzuki. Translated by Ruth A. Kanagy. Kane/Miller, 1988. 32pp. Text in Japanese and English.

The bench in the park could be anywhere, but the people are Japanese and the scenes are from Japan today. The story follows the bench from morning until night, showing all the people, young and old, who pass it or sit on it or maintain it. The tale is printed in small text.

Modern urban Japan has a Western look that is well represented here. Vignettes, double-page spreads, even a couple of pages of comic-strip sequences are rendered in realistic line drawings and dilute watercolors. The changing colors from dawn to night make a circle that encloses a lively collection of mini-dramas. K-Grade 3.

Japanese Americans

Ken Mochizuki, **Baseball Saved Us**. Illustrated by Dom Lee. Lee & Low, 1993. 32pp.

After a note on the U.S. government's internment of all people of Japanese descent in camps in 1942, the author takes us to a desert camp with a young boy who tells his story. In the boredom of camp life, baseball gives his life some focus, and the boy even helps win a game. When the war is over and the family returns home, the boy is shunned and called names when he tries to play on the school baseball team. But through baseball he finally gains acceptance. The story is a satisfying one, told with much information about both the history and the character of the people.

The artist manages to tell the story of prejudice and oppression without resorting to melodramatic cliches. The mixed media include wax, which produces a light source that permeates all scenes, a light drenched with the many browns of

From *Baseball Saved Us* by Ken Mochizuki. Illustrated by Dom Lee. Copyright 1993. Reprinted with permission of Lee & Low.

the "endless desert" of the internment camps. The only blue appears in the sky of the final hopeful scenes. People, in groups and close-ups, are the focus of these illustrations, which have a modified photographic look. Most scenes are full-page but some are smaller. All portray character through action and gesture with attention to details of personality. Grades 2 or 3-6.

Another story of the internment told through the eyes of a child is Yoshiko Uchida's *The Bracelet* (Philomel, 1993) illustrated by Joanna Yardley. The bracelet of the title is the symbol of friendship between a Japanese-American girl and her Caucasian friend.

Kimiko Sakai, **Sachiko Means Happiness**. Illustrated by Tomie Arai. Children's Book Press, 1990. 32pp.

Sachiko's name means happiness in Japanese. She shares this name with her grandmother, who lives with her family. The once-loving grandmother has become so strange that Sachiko does not like taking care of her until she realizes that her grandmother is like a child again. The simply told story is not Japanese, but universal. Any child old enough to understand the problems of Alzheimer's disease can appreciate Sachiko's story.

Visualized as a series of interactions between the two Sachikos, the sequence of scenes fills the right-hand pages and lap over onto the left pages with color and an occasional bit of landscape. Text pages include small vertical panels painted with flowers, fans, and other decorative Oriental devices. Pastels create portraits of the main characters that express the loving relationship possible between caring human beings. Grades 1 or 2-4.

Allen Say, **Grandfather's Journey**. Houghton Mifflin, 1993. 32pp.

Say tells, in simple, brief sentences, the story of his grandfather's trip "to see the world" when he was a young man. He explored America's deserts, prairies, cities, rivers and mountains, meeting people along the way. He married his childhood sweetheart in Japan and brought her back to live in San Francisco, his favorite American place. Later he is drawn back to Japan and although he remembers California fondly, the second World War makes return impossible. Say tells of his own birth and subsequent trip to see the California his grandfather had so fondly described. Succinctly he has summarized here the complex emotions of an immigrant torn between the old country and the new.

Each page has a thinly framed picture and caption-like text

From *Grandfather's Journey* by Allen Say. Copyright 1993. Reprinted with permission of Houghton Mifflin.

below. The illustrations are portraits of people and landscapes. The watercolors are exploited to emphasize their transparencies, allowing the white paper to unify the shapes in ways that seem as if all is seen through memory. Frozen poses seem a collection of old photographs, reproduced lovingly. The painting of Say's mother as a child holding a blond-haired doll is perhaps most symbolic of the author's bi-culturalism, a message also delivered subtly in the sequence of pictures. K or Grades 1-5.

Related Background Materials

Sheila Hamanaka, **The Journey: Japanese Americans, Racism, and Renewal**. Orchard, 1990. 40pp.

Episodes dealing with the events from the early years of World War II when the Japanese population was "detained" in camps to the present outcries against any possible repetition have been incorporated by Hamanaka into a 25-foot mural. The book reproduces sections of the mural.

Ykio Tsuchiya, **Faithful Elephants: A True Story of Animals, People and War**. Illustrated by Ted Lewin. Translated by Tomoko Tsuchiya Dykes. Houghton, 1988. 32pp.

The author first told this story of the tragic wartime fate of the animals in the Tokyo zoo in 1951. It is read aloud every year in Japan, to recall this small part of the horrors of war. Dramatically and accurately illustrated by Ted Lewin, this is a book to use with care because of its emotional impact.

Naomi Wakan, **Reading about Japan: A Bibliography of Japanese Children's Literature**. Vancouver: Pacific-Rim, 1993. paper. 32pp.

Annotates 200 English language children's books with Japanese people or their culture as a central theme. This publisher is also a source for material about Asian cultures.

Ruth Wells, **A to Zen: A Book of Japanese Culture**. Illustrated by Yoshi. Picture Book Studio, 1992. 24pp.

Using an alphabet-book format, the author introduces many aspects of contemporary Japanese life: geography, history, art, architecture, religion, food, money, and calligraphy. The item described in text on each large page is realistically illustrated in a batik technique. The book is to be read "back to front" in Japanese style. Grades 2-6.

Some books dealing with Hiroshima (if you choose to do so) are:

Junko Morimoto, **My Hiroshima**. Viking, 1987. 32pp.

The author tells of her personal experience as a child in Hiroshima at the time the atomic bomb was dropped. Pale watercolors outlined in pen are interspersed with photographs. The horrible facts are all here.

Toshi Maruki, **Hiroshima No Pika**. Lothrop, 1980. 32pp.

Told from the point of view of a young child, this book has more text and more information than Morimoto's. It has even greater emotional impact, however, because of the illustrations. They are impressionistic rather than realistic, using bold strokes and intense color. Although both end on a note of hope, use these books with care. Students as young as first grade can understand the words of Morimoto; only their teachers can tell whether they can understand and deal with what happened at Hiroshima.

Eleanor Coerr's *Sadako and the Thousand Paper Cranes* has long been an inspirational story about the Hiroshima experience for readers of chapter books. The book has "inspired" *Sadako* (Philomel, 1993) a handsome picture book illustrated by Ed Young.

A resource book on Japan (in addition to those in the series listed in the general bibliography) is Vicki Cobb's, *This Place Is Crowded: Japan* from the Imagine Living Here series (Walker, 1992. 32pp.). This is a simply written aid to imagining what living in Japan is like, with bits of added information on culture and history. The large illustrations on every page are accurate and informative but undistinguished.

China and Chinese Americans

Original Tales and Folk Tales Evoking the Past

Hans Christian Andersen, **The Nightingale**. Illustrated by Lisbeth Zwerger. Translated from the Danish by Anthea Bell. Picture Book Studio, 1984. 24pp.

The classic tale of the power of the real nightingale over that of the bejewelled artificial bird is a long one, but retold often enough to have become legendary in Western culture, although it is set in ancient China.

Zwerger maintains her understated watercolor style for the illustrations, a subtle approach that particularly suits the restrained Oriental sensibilities, with lots of spaces of nothing but a hint of washed gray or tan. The costumes, architecture, and furniture are period Chinese, and the people are real and convincing in their actions and facial expressions. The fine line drawings that define objects and characters have a deftness reminiscent of some Western Renaissance drawings. For comparison, see Michael Bedard's *The Nightingale* (Clarion, 1992) below. Grades 2-5 or 6.

Jennifer Armstrong, **Chin Yu Min and the Ginger Cat**. Illustrated by Mary Grandpré. Crown, 1993. 32pp.

Set "many years ago in a village near Kunming," this original story rich in description is concerned with the haughty wife of a prosperous man, and how she found what was really important in life. When her husband dies, Chin Yu Min wants no help from anyone, until her money is spent and her possessions are sold. A cat comes to her rescue, catching fish for her to eat and sell, bringing back a good life. When the cat is suddenly gone, Chin Yu Min first just misses his help, but then realizes it is the cat himself that matters. The searching humbles her and she appreciates the cat and her helpful neighbors.

Oranges and yellowish tans dominate the scenes of village life. Each is a stage set with light sources that create shadows that accentuate the unfolding drama. The human characters tend toward caricature; Chin Yu Min's long fingers almost take on a life of their own as they shoo off neighbors or hold a tea cup or stroke the cat. Her face seems carved from wood like some Oriental

From *Chin Yu Min and the Ginger Cat* by Jennifer Armstrong. Illustrated by Mary Crandpré. Copyright 1993. Reprinted with permission of Crown.

theatrical mask that can change expressive modes. There are many touches of China in utensils, coins, and parts of buildings. Full-page scenes face white pages of text that often have story-enhancing vignettes; all tell a tale of human potential with wit and compassion. Grades 2-5.

Michael Bedard, reteller, **The Nightingale**. Illustrated by Regolo Ricci. Clarion/Houghton Mifflin, 1992. 32pp.

This retelling of the Hans Christian Andersen fairy tale is much like the Anthea Bell translation cited above but gives a larger role to the little kitchen maid, which may make it more appealing to children.

Ricci gives the story an elaborate setting, each page crammed with details of gardens and the imperial palace rooms. Costumes are embroidered with stitches one can almost count. Parchment-like panels holding the text are superimposed on the pictures which are sometimes

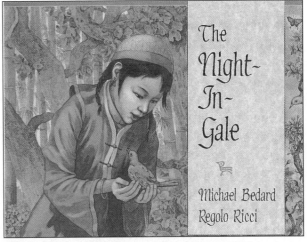

From *The Nightingale* by Michael Bedard. Illustrated by Regolo Ricci. Copyright 1992. Reprinted with permission of Clarion/Houghton Mifflin.

narrow vertical panels and sometimes almost double-page spreads. The watercolor paintings create stagy scenes with actors who tend to overact a bit. This version is a much more physical one depicting all events, whereas Zwerger's creates a more spiritual version. Grades 1 or 2-5.

Demi, **The Magic Boat**. Henry Holt, 1992. 32pp.

This traditional tale is the story of kind, honest young Chang, who rescues an old man from drowning and receives in thanks a tiny boat which magically grows to large size when needed. When a flood threatens, the boat saves

Chang, his mother, and the white cat. Chang in turn rescues an ant, a queen bee, a crane, and tricky Ying, who does not help like the others. When Ying steals the magic boat and takes it to the emperor, Chang's friends and the old man help him retrieve it, despite the tricks of Ying and the emperor.

Demi's tight thin black lines define a world of gabled pavilions, tiny-leafed twisted trees, and a gloriously ornate lacquer-red dragon boat. All surfaces are clean and all action is frozen. There's an echo of the painting on Blue Willow china. All scenes are set in oval shapes framed in a thin gold line, reminiscent of the fan paintings from Chinese history, while gold is used with red for the dominant colors. Grades 1 or 2-4 or 5.

Demi has illustrated many other tales from China. *The Artist and the Architect* (Holt, 1991) uses double-page spreads that house red-framed rectangles and the same meticulous draftsmanship for a tale of jealousy. *Chen Ping and His Magic Ax* (Dodd, 1987), a tale of honesty rewarded, is done with fine line drawings and some watercolor fill-ins and more action than some others. This and *Liang and the Magic Paintbrush* (Holt, 1980, paper 1988) are in smaller format. Liang also outsmarts a wicked emperor. For additional background, *Dragon Kites and Dragonflies: A Collection of Chinese Nursery Rhymes* (Harcourt Brace, 1986) will be of interest to children. This volume's double pages are filled with figures in everyday situations with lots of animal life included that remind one of the scroll paintings from Chinese history.

Elizabeth Hillman, **Min-Yo and the Moon Dragon**. Illustrated by John Wallner. Harcourt Brace, 1992. 32pp.

Although this is an original story, it contains many classic folk-tale elements. In a time when there were no stars, the moon seems to be coming ever closer to the earth. The emperor of China and his wise men seek everywhere for a solution. There is a cobweb stairway to the moon on which people used to climb, bringing diamonds to the dragon living there. An old man suggests that although the stairs are decayed now, a light person might still climb them and deal with the dragon. Little Min-Yo gets the job. She and the dragon work together and put the stars in the sky as part of the solution.

The watercolor paintings, both full-page and double-page spreads, are superimposed on a fading violet border with hints of blossoms, buildings and birds. People are integrated into the dominating landscapes and moonscapes with their gestures emphasizing the narrative flow. The moon dragon is a chubby, blue-eyed fellow with straggly chin whiskers and string mustache. These are gentle pictures that reinforce the story of friendship. K or Grades 1-3 or 4.

Lily Toy Hong, reteller, **How the Ox Star Fell From Heaven**. Whitman, 1991. 32pp.

This old Chinese tale begins "in the beginning" when oxen lived in luxury with the Emperor of All the Heavens, while farmers had to do all the hard work of farming and frequently went days without food. The Emperor decreed that farmers should eat at least once every three days, and sent Ox Star to deliver the message to Earth. By mistake the ox told the farmers they should eat three times each day. The angry emperor banished all oxen to be workers on Earth. Their misfortune makes life sweeter for the people.

Hong achieves a pseudo-cloisonne stylization by filling in spaces created by colored bands with airbrushed acrylic pigments. Thus, the horizontal double-page scenes have an immediate decorative appeal, one that is associated with the traditional Chinese craft of cloisonne. Set in the

From *How the Ox Star Fell from Heaven* by Lily Toy Hong. Copyright 1991. Reprinted with permission of Whitman.

rural countryside, the pictures show people working in the fields as well as several scenes of the abode of the Emperor of All the Heavens. The conceptualizations of the Ox in his silk robe and then "naked" in the fields are particularly imaginative. The illustrations are obviously for fun, but give the flavor of a fairy tale set in another place. Hong's *Two of Everything* (Whitman 1993) is another humorous retelling of a folk tale illustrated in similar style. K or Grades 1-3 or 4.

Caryn Jacowitz, adapter, **The Jade Stone: A Chinese Folktale**. Illustrated by Ju-Hong Chen. Holiday, 1992. 32pp.

Chan Lo, a carver, is given a perfect piece of green-and-white jade by the emperor, who wants a dragon of wind and fire carved from it. But Chan Lo always listens to the stone he carves to hear it tell him what it wants to be. This stone says it should be three carp in a pool, so that's what he carves. The emperor is furious, but waits for his dreams to decide Chan Lo's punishment. The dreams show him that Chan Lo was right. He sends Chan Lo home with honor.

In costume, architecture, and Chinese labels, the illustrations reflect historic China, the one we see in early woodcuts and scrolls. The watercolor paints are absorbed by the soft paper so that the black outlines create the forms. Long, horizontal double pages on a gray background integrate the brief text with the somewhat detailed scenes of the sculptor at work and of the emperor at decision-making. The inclusion of many calligraphed labels or chops to identify characters and objects add significantly to the Oriental feeling. K or Grades 1-3 or 4.

Ju-Hong Chen has also illustrated Winifred Morris's *The Magic Leaf* (Atheneum, 1987), a lengthy text in which costumes and architecture say "long ago and far away" but whose facile watercolors and rather European-looking characters say "here today." For *A Song of Stars: An Asian Legend* adapted by Tom Birdseye (Holiday, 1990), the artist uses a totally different approach, reminiscent of Brian Wildsmith's multicolored extravaganzas. To tell about the myth of the stars separated by the Milky Way, a story that has spread through parts of Asia (with concurrent celebrations), the artist uses pictures that are vignettes spread over the double pages leaving considerable white space for the small print and slight text. Waves are stylized, suggesting Japanese woodcuts. Characters are clothed in patchwork splendor. This is a Westernized, post-cubist visualization of Asia.

Carol Kendall, reteller, **The Wedding of the Rat Family**. Illustrated by James Watts. Macmillan/McElderry, 1988. 32pp.

This old Chinese story is a slightly different version of the Japanese tale in, among others, Eric Kimmel's *The Greatest of All* (Holiday). This version has a lengthy, descriptive text with clever twists. The proud rat family searches for a suitable mate for the youngest daughter, going first to that upon which all life depends, the Sun. The Sun says Black Cloud is more powerful, because he hides Sun. Black Cloud says Wind blows him away, while Wind claims he is stopped by Wall. But Wall won't marry a rat, since rats undermine him. Still, cats are what rats dread, so arrangements are made for a glorious union with cats, with predictable results.

Many parts of the illustrations owe their essence to paintings from Chinese history: the swirling clouds, misty, jutting mountains with tiny buildings at their feet, gnarled tree trunks, the array of costumes. The inventive page layouts and detailed painting style are more in the Western tradition. Watts creates character in his anthropomorphic rats and duplicitous cats. His architecture and the other objects are clearly in the Chinese tradition. The visual drama he produces is an excellent partner for the strong, serio-comic story. Grades 2-5 or 6.

Julie Lawson, reteller, **The Dragon's Pearl**. Illustrated by Paul Morin. Clarion, 1993. 32pp.

In a time long ago a boy named Xiao Sheng works at cutting grass and selling it to support himself and his mother. During a terrible drought, he finds a strange patch of green grass that seems to grow back each day for him to cut. While digging up the grass to transplant it nearer his home, he finds a beautiful pearl. The transplanted grass dies, but the pearl brings rice to the rice jar, and money to the money box. When robbers threaten, Xiao Sheng pops the pearl into his mouth and accidently swallows it. Seized by a terrible thirst, he drinks the river dry, and turns into a dragon. Clouds from his mouth finally bring rain. His mother cries and misses him, but the people honor him and tell his story. Although there is no source specified for this particular story,

From *The Dragon's Pearl* by Julie Lawson. Illustrated by Paul Morin, Reprinted with permission of Clarion.

the author's note gives a great deal of information about the significance of dragons in Chinese iconography and belief, their powers, their qualities, and their difference from dragons in European mythology.

The double-page scene on the jacket and cover sets the stage for mystery. In the mixed-media style of illustration, objects like coins and fabrics are integrated into a cement-like surface that exploits golds and browns with streaks of red. The dragon appears through a window; the pearl is found on the endpapers photographed on a similar mixed-media background. Inside, pages are bordered with a thick, decorated strip across the bottom and thin strips on the other sides of white pages, where the straightforward text is usually set below paintings. Morin's illustrations are naturalistic but use light melodramatically, a bit reminiscent of Rembrandt's later works. Closeups push strong emotional content. If the style does not, the landscapes, interiors, and clothing help define the place as long-ago China. Grades 2-5.

Margaret Mahy, **The Seven Chinese Brothers**. Illustrated by Jean and Mou-sien Tseng. Scholastic, 1990. 40pp.

Mahy tells her brisk, humorous version of this traditional tale using a real person as a character: Emperor Ch'in Shih Huang, 259-210 B.C., who unified China, planned the Great Wall, and may have exploited the workers building it. His end in the story is fiction, however. Each of the brothers has a special power: super hearing, super seeing, extraordinary strength, bones of iron, legs that can grow and grow, the ability never to be too hot, and for the baby brother, the gift of weeping tears big enough to drown a village. Each time the emperor sentences one brother to death, the one who can survive that method of execution replaces him.

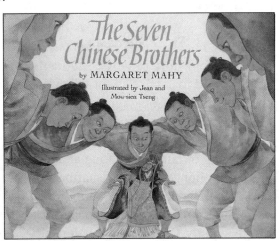

From *The Seven Chinese Brothers* by Margaret Mahy. Illustrated by Jean and Mou-sien Tseng. Copyright 1990. Reprinted with permission of Scholastic.

The Tsengs use a variety of layouts for their watercolor pictures here: vignettes of some of the brothers preparing for the next adventure; full scenes of adventures; multiple panels showing action; parts of objects breaking the thin line borders to emphasize three dimensions; double-page spreads to capture the sweep of a powerful piece of magic. Ornate costumes of royalty and armed soldiers, banners and throne, even the Great Wall, all create the make-believe of ancient China in a dramatic yet light-hearted way. Grades 1 or 2-5.

The Tsengs have illustrated Darcy Pattison's *The River Dragon* (Lothrop, 1991), an original tale of a blacksmith's encounters with a dragon, in similar style.

Winifred Morris, **The Future of Yen-tsu**. Illustrated by Friso Henstra. Atheneum, 1992. 32pp.

Poor young Yen-tsu leaves his father's farm to better his lot, hoping for twists, turns, and surprises in his future. In this traditional tale of old China, Yen-tsu's horse runs away and returns with a mare. The mare tosses Yen-tsu, injuring his leg, so he must limp to the emperor's palace. As in other such tales, an enemy is approaching. Yen-tsu is mistaken for an expected wise man and welcomed with honor. The emperor expects him to answer questions on how to defeat the enemy. As Yen-tsu stammers truthful replies, the emperor interprets his answers so that all turns out well, and Yen-tsu gallops off on a new horse, hoping for further surprises.

Henstra turns his distinctive ink-and-diluted-watercolor style to good use here as he illustrates a time of straw-hatted pedestrians, equestrians, soldiers and an emperor on a high throne. These are designed into scenes that express the temper of the times, posturing rulers, milling crowds, all in the costumes of their ranks. The scratchy ink lines enliven the story while the hints of color simply add eye appeal. Grades 2 or 3-5.

Gerald Rose, **The Fisherman and the Cormorants**. Knopf, 1988. 28pp.

A simply told story of why cormorants are still used to catch fish for fisherman on the Li River. Long ago during hard times, a kind-hearted fisherman gave his small catch to a cormorant whose chicks were dying of hunger. During another time of drought when the fisherman's family is without food, the cormorants bring him fish from another area to repay his generosity. This is the relationship Rose suggests continues today.

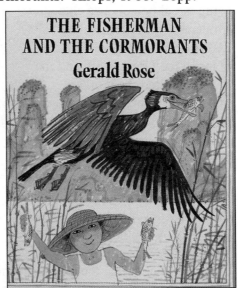

From *The Fisherman and the Cormorants* by Gerald Rose. Copyright 1988. Reprinted with permission of Knopf.

The cover shows a happy fisherman on the banks of a bamboo-fringed river, waving at an almost smiling ascending cormorant. Both are holding fish. Such symbols predict a happy story. The illustrations fulfill the predictions in large and small framed pictures that include considerable local color, such as mountains suggesting those in old Chinese paintings, fishing boats and gear, and costume. Perhaps the humans are treated too comically, particularly the fisherman's three daughters who, by comparison with the more fully developed birds, seem only cartoons. And what are we to make of their toy stuffed panda in this "long ago" story? The cormorants dominate their scenes, their dark bodies against the white-ish sky and river. Be sure to use this only with other books with pictures of Chinese children for students to see along with these. K-Grades 3 or 4.

Meilo So, **The Emperor and the Nightingale**. Bradbury, 1992. 28pp.

This is a simplified retelling of Hans Christian Andersen's fairy tale that works well with younger listeners.

The cover's (front and back) double-page scene shows a roof-topped landscape with emperor and nightingale painted in a manner to emphasize the decorative patterns of fields, flowers, costume, and comic caricature. The hot red arch on the endpapers opens on an intricately presented ceremony of some sort. The same red dominates the title pages ornamented with almost careless brushstroked arabesques. There's a Gilbert and Sullivan operetta feeling to the art, with a cast of thousands and all the props necessary to keep us in the period without taking it too seriously. The black and white toy bird with its nuts and bolts is a stroke of genius. Yet, for all the visual feasting, the illustrations respect the human sensibilities of the narrative as they evoke emotions of contemplation, sorrow, and eventual contentment. Grades 1-4.

Betty L. Torre, reteller, **The Luminous Pearl: A Chinese Folktale**. Illustrated by Carol Inouye. Orchard, 1990. 32pp.

Mai Li, daughter of the Dragon King, wants only a husband who is honest and brave. Hearing of such a man, she goes to meet Wa Jing, but finds his older brother We Ling wishes to marry her as well. To test them, she sends them off to bring her a luminous pearl from the Dragon King of the Eastern Sea, arming each of them with a water-cleaving scythe. On the way, We Ling promises villagers caught in a flood that he will bring them the Dragon King's Golden Dipper in exchange for food and a boat. Wa Jing stops to help the people, also promising them the dipper. From the treasures of the Dragon King, We Ling takes a pearl,

From *The Luminous Pearl* by Betty L. Torre. Illustrated by Carol Inouye. Copyright 1990. Reprinted with permission of Orchard.

but Wa Jing, remembering his promise, gives up his chance at the pearl and the princess to bring the dipper. From the villagers he thus helps, he receives a black pearl which, of course, proves to be the truly luminous winner of the princess. This folk tale has similarities to quest tales to win a princess found in European fairy tales.

Borrowing costumes and some mixed pictorial conventions from old Chinese paintings (wave patterns, weeping willow silhouettes, and mountain landscapes), Inouye combines them in double-page scenes that are sometimes rather naturalistic and sometimes more fantastic. The Dragon King and his courtiers are humans with the heads of sea creatures but his daughter is all human. A bird's-eye view of the Treasure House displays shelves loaded with a delicious melange of tourist kitsch. There is even a hint of early Renaissance painting in the landscape depicting the two brothers' race to the Eastern Sea as the road begins in the lower left corner and winds its way through craggy canyons to the upper right with the shore and distant flooded lands around. Grades 2 or 3-5.

Leong Va, **A Letter to the King**. Translated from the Norwegian by James Anderson. Text in Chinese and English. HarperCollins, 1988. 32pp.

From a 2,000-year-old document he heard about in his childhood, the author retells in simple sentences and large type the tale of a bold girl, who tries to help her unjustly arrested father. Ti Ying and her horse Red Tail go to the capital where her father is imprisoned. Since no one will let her see the king to plead for her father, Ti Ying writes the king a letter telling why her father should be released and offering to go to prison in his place. Failing to get others to deliver it, Ti Ying bravely does the job in person, so impressing the king that he releases her father.

There is an innocence to the illustrations that suggests the way a precocious child might perceive events. Left pages show a small vignette derived from the facing full-page picture. Each miniature is labeled in Chinese and English. Both languages are also used to tell the story, Chinese printed above and English below. Black outline and opaque paint create scenes crowded with tiny figures, in appropriate costume for a 2,000-year-old tale, engaged in activities like using a rice mill or pulling an ornate carriage. There's a feeling of the ancient scroll paintings in the manner in which the picture sequences are designed. Although clothes and buildings are carefully detailed, human faces are given minimal attention. K-Grade 4.

Jay Williams, **Everyone Knows What a Dragon Looks Like**. Illustrated by Mercer Mayer. Four Winds/Macmillan, 1984, Aladdin/Macmillan paper, 1984. 32pp.

When Wild Horsemen threaten the ancient town of Wu on the edge of China, the mandarin's advisors have little advice to offer but to pray to the Great Cloud Dragon. A small, fat, bald man arrives at the city gate and tells Han the gatekeeper that he is the dragon. Han, who's never seen a dragon, takes the man to the mandarin. Although no one in the mandarin's court has ever seen a dragon either, all are sure that they know what one looks like, and the old man isn't it. Only Han is polite enough to offer the man food and drink. In return, the old man shows his power and saves the city.

Mayer's modified Chinese painting style is evident on the jacket where a classical landscape also depicts the dragon and the old man, key characters. The endpapers show a night scene of a similar setting, but now the man is leading us along the path to turn the page. The layout is formal; the right page has a decorative black line border with intricately detailed ink-and-watercolor pictures. The left pages hold the lengthy text and almost always a black ink drawing that illuminates part of the story. Architecture, costumes, artifacts, trees, all suggest a once-upon-a-time China, with the invading horsemen including a touch of Hollywood. The artist's ability to depict apprehensive faces, prancing horses, and traditional trees on loaf-like mountains helps tell a strongly moral tale that has long been popular with children. K or Grades 1-5.

Clara Yen, reteller, **Why Rat Comes First: A Story of the Chinese Zodiac**. Illustrated by Hideo C. Yoshida. Children's Book Press, 1991. 32pp.

This is an original story told to the author by her father. The Jade King in the heavens is curious to meet the animals from Earth, so he sends them invitations to a feast. Of the thousands invited, only twelve arrive. These he honors by naming the twelve years of the calendar cycle after them. But both Rat, because he is clever, and Ox, because he is strong, want to come first. The Jade King asks the children on earth to decide. They choose Rat, who has had himself made large as well as clever. The text is simple, printed in large bold type. Notes inside and on the cover further explain the animal years and signs.

The full-page illustrations exude a vitality created by broken black lines, which outline figures, and colored pencils. The scenes suggest rather than depict environments; the space is so crowded with animals and the court figures that there is little room for much else. Faces are flat with wispy beards; costumes hint at a Chinese theater setting. The style seems influenced by one strand in the tradition of Oriental drawing. K or Grades 1-3 or 4.

Laurence Yep, **The Butterfly Boy**. Illustrated by Jeanne M. Lee. Farrar, Straus, 1993. 32pp.

Yep has used the writings of Chuang Tzu, a Chinese philosopher of the 4th century B.C., to write a deceptively simple but really very enigmatic, poetic tale of a boy who "dreamed he was a butterfly, and, as a butterfly, he always dreamed he was a boy." Dreaming gets him into problematic situations, which he manages to soar above. Neither praise nor blame changes his faith, nor his ability to flit from the snow to blossoming trees and summer meadows.

The duality of viewpoint is visualized in double-page scenes that frequently have a boxed vignette superimposed on them. For example, when an invading army marches across the landscape, the boy's vision of a centipede is illustrated in a red rectangle that covers part of the leader's horse. Opaque paints depict a generalized landscape, mostly with undefined backgrounds and figures more symbolic than realistic. Costumes, a few artifacts and bits of architecture suggest ancient China. The blossoming plum tree and other flowers also contribute to the sense of nature's magical forces that are so influential on the boy's dual personality. Grades 3-6.

Ed Young, **Red Thread**. Philomel, 1993. 32pp.

This story of an ambitious young man named Wei who wants a matchmaker to arrange his marriage to the daughter of a famous general is based on the customs of ancient China. A strange old man tells Wei that a red thread links couples together when they are born and his future bride is only three years old now. When Wei is shown the poor, ugly girl, he pays his servant to kill her. This immoral act, however distant the location, certainly will require some class discussion. Years later Wei marries a governor's beautiful daughter, who always wears a flower seed between her brows. Of course, the seed covers the scar of her stabbing when she was three years old. The predicted destiny has come to pass.

Pastels and watercolor lines convert each double-page scene into a sensual event. Sometimes we get a close-up, like that of the old man, all bluish-purple body with greenish face against a yellow background. On other spreads there are outlines of buildings or crowds touched with bits of colors. Sometimes scale is used to show human insignificance in the larger environment. A horizontal red line near the bottom of each page separates the story text from the pictures, a "red thread." Here's a work where seeing is feeling and hearing, decidedly Chinese by specificity in buildings, by suggestion in clothing. Grades 2 or 3-6.

Young uses pastels similarly in Margaret Leaf's legend-based *Eyes of the Dragon* (Lothrop, 1987). The dragon here is frightening, with Dracula-like fangs, a good story for older students.

Of the many other books Ed Young has illustrated with Asian settings, two retellings are particularly effective: Ai-Ling Louie's *Yeh-Shen: A Cinderella Story from China* (Philomel, 1982) and Young's own *Lon Po Po: A Red-Riding Hood Story from China* (Philomel, 1989) a Caldecott Award Winner. For Yeh-Shen, Young divides each page into two vertical panels with thin red borders. Some house the text, while some try to contain the illustrations. Mixed media, mostly pastels, create the characters in proper period dress, but there are no detailed scenes. Rather there are swirls of color across boxes that on close inspection take on a significant fish shape. *Lon Po Po*, using similar page dividers and mixed media, employs intense colors and even less detail to create its emotional impact.

Taiwan (Formosa) Contemporary

Valerie Reddix, **Dragon Kite of the Autumn Moon**. Illustrated by Jean and Mou-sien Tseng. Lothrop, 1991. 32pp.

The tradition of celebrating Kite's Day, the author's note suggests, came from China to Formosa with early settlers. Tad-Tin is accustomed to flying the special kite his grandfather makes him every year for the holiday. Tradition says that if the string is cut, the kite will carry misfortunes away. But this year, Tad-Tin's grandfather is sick and the kite is unfinished. The only kite Tad-Tin has to fly is the magnificent dragon kite that grandfather made for his birth, which he is reluctant to let go. But he feels he must try to fly the heavy kite and perhaps have grandfather's sickness fly away with it. Does Tad-Tin really see a live dragon when he succeeds? Perhaps that is why grandfather is better when Tad-Tin returns from his night adventure.

Double-page scenes that completely fill the spaces are painted naturalistically with an eye for the furniture and clothes of modern rural Taiwan. The rather restrained illustrations depicting the earthbound family life are juxtaposed with five action-packed, visually inventive scenes of the dragon kite's flight. Grades 1 or 2-4 or 5.

Chinese Americans

Paul Yee, **Roses Sing on New Snow: A Delicious Tale**. Illustrated by Harvey Chan. Macmillan, 1991. 32pp.

As in his collection of stories *Tales from Gold Mountain* (Macmillan, 1989), Yee draws on the traditions of the Chinese immigrants in this tale of a Chinatown restaurant at the turn of the century. Its reputation for fine food comes from Maylin's hard work in the kitchen. But she never hears the compliments because her father tells everyone that his two lazy sons do the cooking. When the governor of South China visits, each restaurant prepares a specialty. Maylin creates the dish of the title. The governor likes it so much that he wants to learn how it is made so he can take it back for the emperor. Maylin is finally credited with the cooking but she shows that food creation, like a painting, can never be completely duplicated.

The illustrations tell a more complex tale than the words, a story replete with details of Chinese cooking and life in a turn-of-the-century Chinatown. It takes a variety of page layouts to encompass the serio-comic tale of a heroic but obedient daughter and her piggish brothers. Watercolors depict the street life as well as tables bearing the variety of foods we associate with Chinese cuisine. Chan picks points of view which add force to this melodrama; for example, the extreme close-up of the governor's unhappy face or the double-page setting of the cooking contest. One can almost smell the food. Grades 1-4.

For more about turn-of-the-century immigrants from China, children can read Eleanor Coerr's story of a boy and his grandfather in a mining town, *Chang's Paper Pony* (Harper, 1988), an easy reader illustrated by Deborah Kogan Ray.

In *Emma's Dragon Hunt* (Lothrop, 1984), Catherine Stock tells about a grandfather, newly arrived from China, who first worries his granddaughter with tales of dragons but then reassures her. Stock's illustrations are Western style watercolors.

Kate Waters and Madeline Slovenz-Low's *Lion Dancer: Ernie Wan's Chinese New Year* with photographs by Martha Cooper (Scholastic, 1990) allows young Ernie to tell about his excited preparations to perform his first Lion Dance. Being part of the undulating lion in the Chinese New Year celebration in New York City's Chinatown is the culmination of his tale. He also gives us factual information about his life as a Chinese American, attending both regular and Chinese school, maintaining some ancient customs, cooking a traditional festival feast in a modern kitchen. The clear photographs are full color. A Chinese lunar calendar and horoscope are included.

Students from grades 2-6 should find *El Chino* (Houghton, 1990) Allen Say's large-format biography of Bong Way "Willie" Wong, the first Chinese-American bullfighter, of great interest.

Background Book on China

Philip Steele, **Journey through China**. Troll, 1991. 32pp.

Briefly covers some history plus important facts on China today. Small but clear color photographs or drawings on every page. A map at the beginning shows areas covered on the journey. Key facts in a Fact File and a Calendar/ Time Chart are included. Grades 2 or 3-6.

Korea and Korean Americans
Original Tales and Folk Tales Evoking the Past

Shirley Climo, **The Korean Cinderella**. Illustrated by Ruth Heller. HarperCollins, 1993. 48pp.

This Cinderella, called Pear Blossom, has a step-mother and step-sister who work her very hard, dress her in rags, and call her Pigling. When they ask her to do impossible tasks, like fill a jar that has a hole in it, or polish every grain in a sack of rice, she gets help from frogs and birds. Step-mother and sister are furious. Pear Blossom receives help with a final task they have set and is on her way to a festival when she loses her sandal. A young magistrate, struck by her beauty, picks up the lost sandal. When he seeks her at the festival, her step-mother and sister happily think it is to punish her, but he wishes to marry her instead. Climo tells the story, drawn from three of the many traditional versions she discusses in her author's note, with words as elaborate as the pictures.

Clearly Heller has also done her homework, as she tells us in her note, so we are treated to meticulous paintings of many traditional Korean objects: clothes, hats, ornaments, and furniture. There is almost a painful effort to represent such details as sparrow feathers, willow branches and crickets, while she creates more general shapes for human figures. The double-page scenes thus combine realism with bands of purely decorative ornamentation and stylized flowers and animals. The scene of acrobats and musicians woven together with white swirling ribbons tells us much about instruments, costumes and actions in a frenetic, dream-like way. Along with the many conventional versions of Cinderella with which to compare this, the author has done an *Egyptian Cinderella* (HarperCollins), which is discussed in the section on Egypt. Grades 1 or 2-4 or 5.

Oki S. Han and Stephanie Haboush Plunkett, adapters, **Sir Whong and the Golden Pig**. Illustrated by Oki S. Han. Dial, 1993. 32pp.

When growing up in Korea, Han's father told her many traditional tales. This lively adaptation of one of them tells of a well-loved, wealthy Sir Whong who lived long ago in Korea. One spring a stranger comes asking to borrow a lot of money. He says it is for medicine for his sick mother, and leaves a golden pig as security. Not only is the pig not real gold, but the stranger is smug about having fooled Sir Whong. Clever Sir Whong, realizing the trick, puts out word that he has lost the pig. When the stranger brings the borrowed money back, hoping to gain high reimbursement for the lost pig, Sir Whong simply takes the money due him and returns the now "found" bogus pig.

The cover illustration introduces the two main characters and also sets the visual stage for the costume-period drama. Watercolors are used in a variety of page layouts. Some describe village life with its many activities in double-page scenes that bleed off the edges. Others set the action inside ornate borders. Each is replete with objects of the time like those seen in museums today. Figures are presented naturalistically in hues and ensembles that express a genuine sense of humanity. Even the villain is dealt with gently. The text is integrated in a variety of unobtrusive ways, giving a sense of unity. The authors have included some notes on ancient Korean money, writing and wedding festivals, like that at which Sir Whong announces his "loss" of the pig. Grades 1 or 2-4.

Anne Sibley O'Brien, adapter and illustrator, **The Princess and the Beggar: A Korean Folktale**. Scholastic, 1993. 32pp.

Many years ago, says this traditional tale, the king grew so tired of the incessant weeping of his sensitive youngest daughter that he threatened to marry her off to Pabo Ondal, the wild beggar who lives in a cave. The princess withdrew to her studies until she was sixteen. Then she refuses the marriage the king has arranged for her, saying she would as soon marry Pabo Ondal as he had threatened. Her enraged father banishes her to the beggar. Surprisingly, the two learn from and care for each other. After some time, the princess sends Ondal as a commoner to compete in the Festival of the Hunt, where he does surprisingly well, but still hides his identity. Finally, in the Festival of the Scholars, when he writes a prize-winning poem although he is supposed to be illiterate, the truth is revealed. The king offers his favor, but the couple ask only to serve him when needed, for they are content. In a note, the author explains the setting and the time period she has chosen plus other information about the culture.

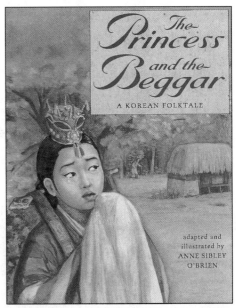

From *The Princess and the Beggar* by Anne Sibley O'Brien. Copyright 1993. Reprinted with permission of Scholastic.

There are several visual devices used to produce a sense of an ancient Korean place. Endpapers are decorated with symbolic roundels. The covers display a main character in a native setting, while an opening double-page aerial view lays out a meandering river and a walled village below craggy mountains. The story unfolds on horizontal and vertical panels with text on white panels. Pastels create naturalistic scenes more to evoke emotion than to provide explicit details: the blurry riders through the forest tell enough about the subject while they make us feel the speed of the chase. Costumes and architecture provide the visual aspects for the cultural context. Grades 1 or 2-4 or 5.

Nami Rhee, **Magic Spring: A Korean Folktale**. Putnam/Whitebird, 1993. 32pp.

Rhee retells and illustrates a folk tale told to her as a child in Seoul. A poor, hardworking, childless couple are taunted by their rich and greedy neighbor. One day the old man follows an elusive bluebird to a refreshing spring with magic power, which turns him into a young man again. Of course he brings his wife to drink as well. When the neighbor demands to know how they became young, he seeks out the spring but drinks to excess. The couple go to find him when he doesn't return, but he has turned into a crying baby. They are delighted to make a happy family for the baby.

      Rice paper-toned paper combines with the brushed black lines and transparent watercolors to present the feel of Oriental pictures. The economy of line and color and the expressive energy of each stroke add to the effect. Facial features are exaggerated, landscapes are simplified almost to the point of abstract symbols. The English text with bits of accompanying excerpts in Korean is comfortably accommodated in corners of each double-page scene. Information on the relationship of the story to the traditional Korean values, as well as details on the creation of the illustrations, are included in an introductory note. K or Grades 1-3 or 4.

      For the very young, Holly H. Kwon has retold *The Moles and the Mireuk: A Korean Folk Tale* (Houghton Mifflin, 1993) in simple language and large print. This version of the Oriental story of the mouse or rat seeking the best husband for his daughter (see above) is illustrated by Woodleigh Hubbard, whose watercolors here owe much more to Miro than to traditional Korean art. His highly abstract shapes are mostly simple symbols of objects painted in arbitrary colors. Only the statue is Korean.

Korea Today

We have no picture books about life in Korea today. Patricia McMahon's *Chi-Hoon: A Korean Girl* (Boyds Mills, 1993), illustrated with color photographs by Michael F. O'Brien, does give children insight into this country through the words of an eight-year-old girl telling about the events of a week in her life.

Korean Americans

Min Paek, **Aekyung's Dream**. Children's Book Press, 1988. 24pp. Text in English and Korean.

Drawing upon her own experiences and those of other newcomers, the author tells of Aekyung's feelings as a stranger in school, teased by other students, thinking even the birds are singing in English. Inspired by her aunt's return from a visit to Korea and a dream about 15th-century King Sejong, Aekyung gains the strength to learn English and help others as well.

      Thin black lines define highly simplified shapes, a very few of which represent traditional Korean costumes and a building. Stylized figures stiffly posed in either empty spaces or sterile settings show Aekyung's efforts to adapt to her new life in the United States. The illustrations try as much to deal with her feelings as to visualize events. Grades 1 or 2-4.

Sook Nyul Choi's *Halmoni and the Picnic* (Houghton Mifflin, 1993) illustrated by Karen M. Dugan is a simple but long text describing young Yunmi's concern when her grandmother agrees to chaperone her class picnic. Yunmi fears the others will not accept the grandmother's traditional Korean dress or cooking. Of course, all goes well. The illustrations portray the kids of today as well as the traditional costume of the grandmother. For grades K-3 or 4.

Vietnam and Vietnamese Americans

Original Tales and Folk Tales Evoking the Past

Sherry Garland, **Why Ducks Sleep on One Leg**. Illustrated by Jean and Mou-sien Tseng. Scholastic, 1993. 32pp.

This long but humorous *pourquoi* tale begins long ago in Vietnam, when animals could talk and spirits were everywhere. The ruler then was the Jade Emperor. The only unhappy creatures were three ducks. Their life was hard and they were teased because they each had only one leg. They decide to petition the Jade Emperor for help, and so begin a long journey. When they reach the hut of the village guardian, he refuses to take their petition to the emperor. But he agrees to give them three extra gold legs from an incense burner if they will guard them carefully. This they do by tucking them safely under their wings each night. This custom is then adopted by other ducks as a comfortable way to sleep.

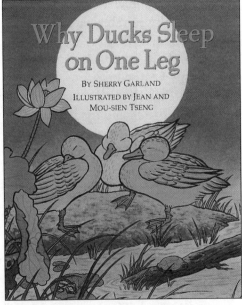

Heavy black outlines filled in with opaque watercolors create a rather static quality, a sequence of frozen tableaux. Each double-page scene contains some bits of historical artifacts: building, furniture, brush and ink, even a dragon. These unbordered illustrations are designed to attract our eyes by exploiting textured washes for skies and ground and loading the scenes with actors, large blossoming plants, or cavorting animals. These glib paintings hint at their Oriental roots while giving some specific details. The author's note gives a brief history of Vietnam and discusses the ancient village life she has depicted in the story. Grades 1 or 2-4.

From *Why Ducks Sleep on One Leg* by Sherry Garland. Illustrated by Jean and Mou-sien Tseng. Copyright 1993. Reprinted with permission of Scholastic.

Mary B. Hill, reteller, **Kim Tong and the Money Lender: A Folktale from Vietnam**. Illustrated by Nancy Malick. Bookmakers Guild (Lakewood, Colorado), 1990. 32pp.

The author's introduction is a plea for human understanding and a bit simplistic in its explanations, giving little information and no source for her story. The tale of clever young Kim Tong and how he outwits the disagreeable Moneylender is a humorous though wordy one. When he explains his riddle-like words to the Moneylender, Kim Tong is promised that his father's debt will be canceled, with a fly cited as the witness. Of course the Moneylender denies the promise, so the two must take the case to the Great Mandarin who rules the country. There the Moneylender is tricked by Kim Tong into admitting the truth.

   The clothing and the hints of buildings suggest Southeast Asia, but the mixed media technique used to picture the rural life style is more universal. Whirls for clouds and swirls for foliage in an undulating landscape create agitation. The conventionalized figures seem designed for decorative effect or for slapstick humor rather than for a picture of old Vietnam. Grades 1 or 2-4.

Vietnam Today

Eva Boholm-Olsson, **Tuan**. Illustrated by Pham van Don. Translated by Dianne Jonasson. R & S Books, 1986. 24pp.

The author, who has lived in northern Vietnam, tells of the life of a five-year-old boy today. Young Tuan chooses to go to his grandmother's instead of the care center while his mother works. He then goes to the rice fields with his cousin, but while walking along is bitten by a stray dog. The crisis because of the possibility of rabies and the shortage of available vaccine plus his mother's anxiety add a difficult note to this otherwise simple but wordy story for young children. Fortunately all ends well with the celebration of the traditional Children's Festival.

   Although the illustrations are naturalistic in depicting the rice fields of a rural countryside and the people going about their mundane activities, the use of silk as a surface makes the paintings appear as if they were done on blotting paper. All forms seem to blur together in a misty atmosphere. Where the text is integrated into double-page scenes there is a good sense of narrative flow, but most often the smaller illustrations are combined in pages with text in white spaces. These pages look more like a textbook, particularly because of the detailed information they provide. K or Grades 1-4.

Vietnamese Americans

Sherry Garland, **The Lotus Seed**. Illustrated by Tatsuro Kiuchi. Harcourt Brace Jovanovich, 1993. 32pp.

The story is written as if told by a Vietnamese-American girl recounting her grandmother's tale of the lotus seed she saved from a pod in the Imperial garden the day she, as a young girl, saw the emperor cry when he gave up his throne. The grandmother hid the seed through the years when she married, saw war come, fled in a small boat, and arrived in this strange new country. The girl tells how her grandmother weeps when her little brother steals the precious seed. A lotus grows where he planted it, with a seed pod so that the grandmother and each grandchild can have a seed to remember. The text is very simple, the print large, but the history and issues raised are complex. The author's note on Vietnamese history will help.

The sequence of subtly framed oil paintings on cream-colored pages tells the main events along with the brief text. The pictures supply detailed information about the adventures the words leave out: the fires as the grandmother runs; the American kitchen with seven family members hard at work; the objects on the altar where the lotus seed is hidden. Sympathy is generated by the elegance of the design as well as by the choice of limited colors that suffuse each scene with softly focused light. Grades 1 or 2-4 or 5.

Tran-Khanh-Tuyet, **The Little Weaver of Thai-Yen Village**. Illustrated by Nancy Hom. Children's Book Press, 1987. 24pp. Text in English and Vietnamese.

The war in which her father has been fighting for eight years comes to Hien's village in the rice fields, killing her mother and grandmother and sending her to the hospital. In her depression she is comforted by a dream of the spirit bird Me-Linh, who has traditionally inspired her people in time of war. She needs an operation for which she must go to the United States, a place she fears because its people had brought the war to her village. Although the operation is a success, Hien still misses her country. Until she can return, she weaves the spirit bird image into blankets to be sent back to her people. The author's note further explains her experiences with children like Hien in 1969 and 1970, and since. This difficult story requires introduction with historical background.

There is also a harshness to the unmodulated saturated enamel-like colors used to fill in the black lines that outline all shapes in the illustrations. Borders of solid colors contain the bilingual texts and scenes of both village life during the war and Hien's life in this country. Shapes are simplified almost to the point of jigsaw puzzle pieces, while gestures are linear embellishments on the flat surfaces. The impression is one of a series of posters rather than of the arts or crafts of the area. Grades 2 or 3-5.

Background Books

Diane Hoyt-Goldsmith, **Hoang Anh: A Vietnamese American Boy**. Photos by Lawrence Migdale. Holiday House, 1992. 32pp.

A young boy describes his new life in America, including the customs and rituals his family have brought with them from Vietnam. Clear photographs, a glossary, and a map all help bring the culture to life. Grades 3-6, younger for the pictures.

Michele Maria Surat, **Angel Child, Dragon Child**. Illustrated by Vo-Dinh
Mai. Raintree, 1983, Scholastic paper, 1989. 36pp.

The moving story of a young girl from Vietnam trying to adjust to the cruelty
of the teasing in school. All finally is well. The lengthy text and notes offer
much information while the competent color pastel illustrations convey
emotion as well as background facts. Grades 2 or 3-4 or 5.

Laos: Folktale

Blia Xiong, **Nine-in-One Grr! Grr!: A Folktale from the Hmong People of
Laos**. Adapted by Cathy Spagnoli. Illustrated by Nancy Hom. Hardback and
Paper. Children's Book Press, 1989. 32pp.

In this tale heard during the author's childhood in Laos, Tiger goes to visit the
great god Shao in the sky to find out how many cubs she will have. Shao tells
her "nine each year," but only if she can remember the words. Tiger, whose
memory is bad, makes up the song of the title to sing all the way home so she
won't forget. Bird, unhappy at the thought of all those tigers, distracts Tiger
long enough to substitute "one in nine." This keeps the tiger population down
in this simply told, large print story.

      Silk screen has been used to translate the needlework of the story cloths
which have emerged as a new form of the traditional Hmong craft. Thus each
illustration is a scene with a distinctive and multiframed border, thin bands of
color and a thicker band with geometric patterns. The scenes use symbols,
stylized animal and floral shapes, set onto colored backgrounds, which are
mostly without horizon or ground. Costumes and a building derive from the
culture. The palette of saturated blues, red, and greens is consistent with both
the needlework and the land. Similar work comes from the Chung Mai area of
Thailand and is frequently found in import shops. K-Grade 4.

Cambodia/Kampuchea

An Original Tale Evoking the Past

Jeanne M. Lee, **Silent Lotus**. Farrar, Straus, 1991. 32pp.

Inspired by the decorations on the 12th-century temple at Angkor Wat,
Vietnamese-born Lee has written a relatively simple story of a girl named
Lotus, born long ago in Kampuchea. Lotus could not hear or speak but grew
up happily dancing with the herons and cranes by the lake. She was lonely,
however, because other children would not play with her. Her mother and
father take her to the temple in the city to see if the gods will show them how to
help her. When Lotus sees the temple dancers and begins to dance, the king
and queen send her to learn the traditional dances. She becomes the most
famous dancer in the Khmer kingdom.

      The utter smoothness of all surfaces (ground, water, sky, walls) gives
the opaque paintings a mythic quality. Like the stone reliefs of the temples,
these are pictures frozen in time, created for their decorative esthetic impact as
well as for information about an ancient kingdom. Costumes, jewelry,
architecture are all crisply rendered. On most of the text pages Lee has used a

soft black pencil to produce pseudo stone reliefs with figures relating to the story line. K or Grades 1-4.

Lina Mao Wall's *Judge Rabbit and the Tree Spirit: A Folktale from Cambodia*, adapted by Cathy Spagnoli (Children's Book Press, 1991), bilingual in English and Khmer, is a simply told, lively story of the traditional character and how he solves the dilemma of which husband is real and which is a tricky spirit. Unfortunately Nancy Hom's illustrations are not as competent as the tale itself.

Background Book

Nancy Price Griff, **Where the River Runs**. Little, Brown, 1993. 70pp. Experiences of a Cambodian immigrant family, illustrated with photographs by Richard Howard, are really told for older children, but the photos make the book accessible to younger students.

India
Original Tales and Folk Tales Evoking the Past

Marcia Brown, **Once a Mouse...: from ancient India, a fable cut in wood.** Scribners/Macmillan, Aladdin paper, 1961. 32pp.

After saving a mouse from being snatched by a crow, a hermit turns him into a cat to keep him from being eaten by one. He turns the cat into a dog when another dog frightens the cat. Finally he turns the dog into a tiger, who becomes so proud that he threatens the hermit. The hermit then returns the tiger to mouse again. This very simple story, told in few words, still offers much to discuss.

The three-color woodcuts exploit the medium's powerful forms in their rough minimal chiseling and near-miss overlapping of the olive, red, and gold inks. Probably the only objects that convey a sense of India are the old bearded man in turban and *dhoti* and the tiger. From the endpapers with their leaping deer and other animals and the abstracted forest setting in which the hermit tends to the animals' needs, there is a spiritual quality that seems to evoke some Indian values. Perhaps it's the manner in which the hermit squats to contemplate or in the majestic magic of his countenance as he changes the tiger back into a mouse. Conveying concepts from another culture is sometimes possible through such spare esthetic means. K or Grades 1-4.

Gloria Kamen, **The Ringdoves; from the Fables of Bidpai**. Atheneum, 1988. 32pp.

From original fables written around 300 B.C. in India, Kamen has selected this story of animal friendship. After following a flock of netted doves to the burrow of Zirak the mouse and seeing him gnaw them free, a crow befriends Zirak. He even finds them a safer place to live near another friend, the tortoise. A gazelle soon makes the friendship a foursome. When the friends help the gazelle out of a hunter's trap, the hunter catches the tortoise. Then the friends trick the hunter out of his catch. Discouraged, the hunter moves to another area, leaving the four friends in peace.

Hints of illustrated books from 15th- and 16th-century India appear in some treatment of the trees, the figure of the hunter, and in the title page's frieze of turtles and mounted warriors. The floral arabesques of the endpapers also contribute to the effect. The text is set on almost every page in double bordered lines of blue and gold. The watercolor illustrations, sometimes full page but frequently vignettes, mix rather stylized trees with more naturalistic renderings of animals and hunter in typical costume. Grades 2-6.

Kristina Rodanas, **The Story of Wali Dad**. Lothrop, 1988. 32pp.

Basing her tale on an Andrew Lang retelling of a fairy tale, Rodanas has changed a fairy magic part of the story and has set it in an imaginary, mystical India of long ago. Old Wali Dad, having earned some money from his hay-cutting, buys a gold bracelet. He decides to send it to a kind and beautiful woman he has heard about, the Princess of Khaistan, via his friend the merchant. The princess sends beautiful silk in return. Wali Dad, not knowing what to do with such silk, sends it to an honorable prince, again with the merchant. The prince sends back some horses, which Wali Dad sends in turn to the princess. She returns mules laden with silver, which he sends to the prince, and so it goes in this richly told story until all ends happily with the wedding of the prince and princess.

The portrait of Wali Dad on the jacket and cover could be your guide to the wonders of Agra today. Within, paintings framed in red and blue lavishly detail a sari's pattern, a jewelled necklace's gems, a racing horse's mane, the ripples in an Oriental rug unfolding as it is displayed in the bustling market; all convey an exotic sense of romantic India, a make-believe place where an old haycutter can play matchmaker for a princess. The colors are intense, leaving no tube unsqueezed, as the scenes are overrun with the generosity of all involved, including the illustrator. Grades 2-6.

Aaron Shepard, **Savitri: A Tale of Ancient India**. Illustrated by Vera Rosenberry. Whitman, 1992. 40pp.

The loyal and clever Princess Savitri's story is part of the Hindu epic *Mahabharata*. She chooses to wed Satyavan, who has no kingdom, lives with his father in a simple hermitage, and is doomed to die within a year. When Yama, god of death, comes for Satyavan, Savitri follows after, gaining concessions from Yama and finally cleverly forcing him to release her husband's spirit.

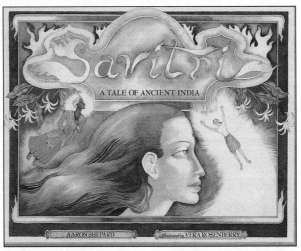

From *Savitri: A Tale of Ancient India* by Aaron Shephard. Illustrated by Vera Rosenberry. Copyright 1992. Reprinted with permission of Whitman.

Stylistically the figures, gestures, facial expressions, and surrounding details of landscape and artifact suggest aspects of historical illustrated books from India. Gold frames enclose the text and facing page of illustration. These pictures are frequently overpainted, as parts of the theatrically designed scenes break out of confinement. Ink and transparent watercolors create decorative foliage, peaceful-looking animals, and a starkly stylized environment for the simply told story. Grades 1 or 2-6.

Milo Cleveland's *Adventures of Rama* (Smithsonian, 1983) is a splendid collection with illustrations from a 16th-century Mughal manuscript.

Madhur Jaffrey's *Seasons of Splendour: Tales, Myths & Legends of India* (Atheneum, 1985) gives 125 pages of the wonderful heritage of Hindu Indian folklore. Michael Foreman's watercolors are a fine addition.

Traditional Tales with Nontraditional Illustrations

Brian Gleeson, **The Tiger and the Brahmin**. Illustrated by Kurt Vargo. Rabbit Ears, 32pp.

The story of a jackal who saves the wise man from being eaten by the tiger. Grades 2-5.

Margaret Hodges, **The Golden Deer**. Illustrated by Daniel San Souci. Scribners, 1992. 32pp.

From the Indian classic *The Jakata* comes this tale of the Buddha in the shape of a golden deer saving the herd and other animals. Grades 1-4.

Contemporary India

Ruskin Bond, **Cherry Tree**. Illustrated by Allan Eitzen. Caroline House/ Boyds Mills Press, 1991. 32pp.

Young Rakhi's grandfather suggests she plant the seed from one of the cherries she has eaten in the soil of the stony Himalayan foothills of northern India. She watches it grow, cares for it through accidents and insect threats, and grows herself as well. As a young woman, she can enjoy the cherry blossoms with her grandfather and imagine telling her own children the story of the cherry tree. The author, who lives in India, has written this original story about his local area.

Eitzen's combination of patterned cut paper (mostly for Rakhi's clothes) and paints creates scenes that suggest a peaceful bucolic life. The pictures fill the pages while the few lines of text are given comfortable places to tell their story. Both the grandfather and Rakhi are drawn as universally appealing characters. Trees, mountains, and even the weather are treated somewhat abstractly, e.g., the cherry tree spreads like a fan across an azure sky, each almond-shaped leaf set like a jewel on its branch. K or Grades 1-4.

Peter Bonnici, **The Festival**. Illustrated by Lisa Kopper. Carolrhoda, 1985. 32pp.

Arjuna, a young Indian boy from the city, visits his mother's family in a village. He is bored until drawn into the preparations for a temple festival in which he participates with his uncle and the other men. He has an amusingly embarrassing experience, which his family helps him to overcome. Told simply in large print, the tale is based on the author's childhood memories and his visits to India since. Additional notes describe other traditional Hindu festivals.

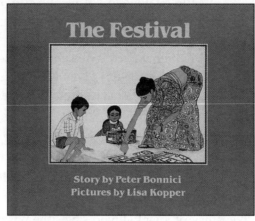

Borderless double pages comfortably accommodate both the simple text and attractive, realistic pictures of life in a contemporary Hindu village. Using blue and brown watercolors, Kopper supplies all sorts of details, from baking cookies on a basic charcoal stove to a scene of the flower-bedecked men dancing around a statue of Ganesha. People are depicted as individuals involved in their daily lives. K-Grade 4.

From *The Festival* by Peter Bonnici. Illustrated by Lisa Kopper. Copyright 1985. Reprinted with permission of Carolrhoda.

Aleph Kamal, **The Bird Who Was an Elephant**. Illustrated by Frane Lessac. Lippincott, 1989. 32pp.

The story describes Bird's progress to the village from the desert, past the river, the street of shops, a stop at the palmist, who tells him he was an elephant in his past life and will be a fish in the next, past beggars, a sacred cow, a wise man, a snake charmer, the train station, the temple, and finally to rest at night in a tree. Nothing happens but everyday life in an Indian village. The author's note discusses the Hindu belief in rebirth, and the Indian words used.

Jaunty opaque painted scenes depict the contemporary Hindu village. Lessac details the men who wander with mat and bowl, the women vendors under their umbrellas, the statues and bells and sticks of incense in the temples. Figures and buildings are rendered simply without modeling, as much for their overall decorative effect as for the conveying of information. Each page is bordered with a different band of color that contains tiny pictures of objects relating to the subject of the illustration. The direct simplicity of the pictures conveys a genuine sense of place. Grades 1-4.

Anni Axworthy's *Anni's Indian Diary* (Whispering Coyote Press, 1992) jauntily describes young Anni's trip through India with her family. Illustrated with sketches and photographs, this is a good introduction to this vast country for children.

Nobel Prize-winning Rabindranath Tagore's poem *Paper Boats* (Caroline House/Boyds Mills Press, 1992) is a fine introduction to this Indian writer for even young children. Although well-done and carefully placed on the pages, cut-paper illustrations by Grayce Bochak of a young boy making and sending off his paper boats unfortunately convey very little of India.

(Unfortunately we have no picture books about Indian Americans.)

Sri Lanka

Original Tales and Folk Tales Evoking the Past

Joanna Troughton, **The Quail's Egg: A Folktale from Sri Lanka (Folktales of the World)** Peter Bedrick, 1988. 32pp.

This cumulative tale begins with an egg, which rolls out of reach of the mother quail. She seeks help from a stone mason to cut away the rock holding it. He will not, nor will the pig trample the mason's rice, nor will the thorny creeper prick the pig, and so on until the quail finds a cat who will catch the mouse and start the chain ending in the egg's liberation.

There is a light-hearted charm to the mixed media, basically watercolor pictures which depict a shrewish mother quail pestering the series of possible helpers. Also shown are the "druthers" of these helpers: the water dreams of being a waterfall, the elephant desires to snare a big bunch of bananas and so forth. There is a simplicity to it all with a design sense that can integrate the evolving text, the quail's pleas, and the daydreams into attractive double pages. The endpapers present each of the characters in repeated small vignettes, to get us in the mood for the fun. K-Grade 3.

Sybil Wettasinghe, **The Umbrella Thief**. Kane/Miller, 1987. 24pp.

This original story takes place in a small Sri Lankan village where the residents had never seen an umbrella. When Kiri Mama discovers umbrellas in a nearby town, he buys one to bring back. But it is mysteriously stolen, as is each one he subsequently buys. He finally tracks them all down, opens a successful umbrella shop with those he finds, and leaves one umbrella for the thief with a funny surprise inside.

It's evident from the wiggly line drawings of people with umbrellas on the endpapers that this is a funny story. Thick black outlines broadly define figures, trees, shops, and ordinary life in the village. Opaque paints supply the colors of the environment and the riot of design of typical costume. Scumbled and overlaid, the paints create a colorful coffee shop with its hanging bananas and rows of glass jars filled with sweets. There is an audacious moonlit scene done all in black and white, and another where the setting sun dabs bright red on forest trees. Of course, caricature is the appropriate style for this laid-back comedy. K or Grades 1-4.

Tibet

Mordicai Gerstein's *The Mountains of Tibet* (Harper, 1987), which grew from his reading of the Tibetan *Book of the Dead*, offers a simple introduction in picture book format to the idea of reincarnation common in Eastern religions.

Australia and New Zealand
Original Tales and Folk Tales Evoking the Past

Stefan Czernecki and Timothy Rhodes, **The Singing Snake**. Illustrated by
Stefan Czernecki. Hyperion, 1993. 40pp.

Long ago, says the legend, Old Man became tired of all the noise the animals
on his island made. He decided to make a musical instrument to honor
whoever developed the most beautiful voice, the winner to be decided in a
contest. Snake decides that Lark has the most beautiful voice, so he swallows
her. When he smiles, the sun strikes her and she begins to sing through his
mouth. All the other animals agree that what they think was Snake's voice is
the best. When asked to sing again, Lark scratches instead until Snake can no
longer bear the pain and coughs her up. Meanwhile, Old Man has begun to
make his instrument in the shape of snake. This becomes the traditional
didgeridoo, further described in the authors' note. And Snake is thereafter
shunned by the other animals

      Some aboriginal peoples of Australia have developed a style of painting
which exploits dots. They make outlines and fill them with dots of color
applied quite methodically. The endpapers show us snakes of different colors,
all dotted. A border encloses text and pictures alike, a broad band that houses
snakes and simply decorative areas of dotted color. Scenes are stylized after
the fashion of much aboriginal painting, using simplified forms, many shown
with characteristic x-rayed bodies, a few with bony remains in their guts. A
brick red, the earth color of the Australian desert, dominates. All is flatly
painted with opaque paints. Western in the design of pages, the book has
illustrations influenced by aboriginal pictures. K-Grade 4.

Rudyard Kipling, **The Sing-Song of Old Man Kangaroo**. Illustrated by John
Rowe. Picture Book Studio, 1990. 28pp.

Kipling's classic tale from Just So Stories about Kangaroo, who got his wish to
be different from all the other animals by being chased all day by Yellow-Dog
Dingo, is presented here in its original, distinctive language. The few
Australian and aboriginal terms used are described in notes at the end of the
story.

      The 12 full-page paintings, with broad white bands that blend with the
facing text pages, are in no way reproductions or recreations in the style of
aboriginal works. But somehow the choice of intense blues, brick red, and
warm tans conveys the feel of the Australian outback. Nqong, the Little God,
is depicted a bit like some of the pictographs seen on cave walls in the outback.
The Australian animal characters are Rowe's own inventions. It's the way
these figures are organized on the sparse landscape, their frequently frenetic
actions and enigmatic pauses that evoke the sense of the mystic from both the
Kipling story and the way of the aboriginals. Grades 2-6.

Deborah Nourse Lattimore, **Punga the Goddess of Ugly**. Harcourt Brace,
1993. 36pp.

"Once not very long ago" on the North Island of New Zealand, twin sisters
Kiri and Maraweia lived with their grandmother, who was teaching them the

Maori ways: the weaving, the songs, the stories, the dances. But the girls need more practice for the haka dance, which must be beautiful. Otherwise they could end up like Mudfish and Lizard in grandmother's legend, stuck like a carving on the lodgepole of Punga the goddess of Ugly. One night Maraweia runs off after making ugly faces. Following her, Kiri sees her sister turned into wood on Punga's lodge, and challenges Punga to let them dance. The beauty of their dance frees Mudfish, Lizard, and finally Maraweia. The girls return to grandmother, who is surprised at the mokos, or chin tattoos, that have magically appeared on their faces.

Lattimore clearly bases her illustrations on the traditional Maori carvings and on the natural history of New Zealand. Her mixed-media watercolors present the intricacies of the carvings and the realistic anatomy of birds, lizards, and flowers. She is also able to reproduce the gestures and facial expressions involving the tongue that characterize one of the fundamental and unique Maori traditions. Punga's tongue is shown to be a formidable object. Also traditional are the mokos the girls find on their chins. This first picture book on the fascinating customs and art of the Maori to reach the United States is a welcome introduction. The author's note, map, and glossary at the end are all helpful additions. Grades 2-6.

Arone Raymond Meeks, **Enora and the Black Crane: An Aboriginal Story**. Scholastic, 1993. 32pp.

Enora and his people live in a beautiful rain forest by a river. All birds are black and white. One day Enora sees a "flickering splash of color" flitting through the trees. He follows it deep into the forest, where he sees the colors touch the feathers of a group of birds. When he returns, no one will believe his tale, so he sets out to find and bring back proof. He kills a crane for this purpose, which is a bad thing to do. Soon he is covered with black feathers. As a bird, he feels he must return to the other birds. The colors stay with them, but he remains black. Meeks tells the story from his cultural heritage simply.

Red pages are clearly not the background we might expect for a rain forest legend. But this hue delivers a visual punch, acting as a fine background for the stylized white-outlined figures and black-and-white birds. Of course there are the traditional dots, mainly yellow but other colors also, used in many ways. Forms suggest many of the visual combinations found in aboriginal paintings, but much of the design is Western. The full-page illustrations

From *Enora and the Black Crane* by Arone Raymond Meeks. Copyright 1993. Reprinted with permission of Scholastic.

face the white pages of text. The final double-page scene of birds makes a stunning climax. Grades 1-4.

Susan Nunes' *Tiddalick the Frog* (Atheneum, 1989) illustrated by Ju-Hong Chen tells an aboriginal folk tale from "long ago in the Dreamtime" (a concept which is difficult for Westerners to understand but essential for any sense of this culture) when a frog drinks all the water in the world. The illustrations, although portraying some native Australian animals, do not otherwise relate to the culture.

Australia Today

Jeannie Baker, **Where the Forest Meets the Sea**. Greenwillow, 1987. 32pp.

In simple language and few words, Baker tells of a boy's visit with his father to a tropical rain forest in North Queensland, Australia. He explores, speculates on the history of the area, and wonders how long it will last unsullied.

The forest is recreated by photographing a variety of materials assembled into low relief scenes. A sandy beach, clear creek, interlaced treetops and intricately convoluted root systems are all represented realistically by very inventive manipulations of natural objects and clay. Then to enhance the illusion, Baker includes ghost-like images of things that the father and son discuss, like the ancient crocodiles and dinosaurs, and the original aboriginal inhabitants. The final scene is of a projected resort development on a deserted cove. These illustrations push the bare-bones text to the furthest reaches of our visual imagination. K or Grades 1-6.

The animals unique to Australia are of great interest to children. Some good light-hearted picture book introductions to these include Kerry Argent's *Wombat and Bandicoot, Best of Friends* (Joy Street/Little Brown, 1988), Mem Fox's *Possum Magic* (Abingdon, 1987) illustrated by Julie Vivas, and Rod Trinca and Kerry Argent's *One Wooly Wombat* (Kane/Miller, 1985) illustrated by Kerry Argent.

Background Books

Additional books about the different countries of Asia are too numerous to mention, and are constantly becoming outdated or replaced by newer editions. A search by the name of the country in any library should bring something useful.

Most libraries will also have books about the art of each country. Ask the librarian for help in searching by subject. A few fine new books replete with color illustrations from Rizzoli's series called Treasures of Asia include *Chinese Painting*, text by James Cahill (1977), and *Indian Painting*, text by Douglas Barrett and Basil Gray (1978). Naomi Noble Richard and Deborah Del Gals's *Asian Art in the Art Institute of Chicago* (Abrams, 1993) offers 120 superb color photographs.

Section 4

The Middle East and North Africa

To move geographically west from Asia along the ancient trade routes is to use a well-traveled road. Just as Alexander the Great carried the Hellenistic culture with his campaigns, and the Moghul conquest of India overlaid its art and culture upon the Hindu and Buddhist traditions, the rise of Islam in the 7th century swept across this area layering a sort of religious and cultural unity upon the many diverse cultures. The conflicts from the underlying differences are constantly making headlines today.

There are large numbers of immigrants to the United States from this part of the world, but their stories are not yet well-represented in picture books. We need more about the lands from which they come as well as documentation of their immigrant experiences for children.

Egypt

Original Tales and Folk Tales Evoking the Past

Shirley Climo, **The Egyptian Cinderella**. Illustrated by Ruth Heller. Crowell, 1989. 32pp.

The author's note tells us that the tale of Rhodopis, first recorded in the first century B.C., is partially fable, but a Greek slave girl with that name did marry a pharaoh in the 6th century B.C. This Cinderella is scorned by the other servants because of her fair skin and hair (an interesting twist for children to discuss). Her master orders special slippers for her because she dances so beautifully. Rhodopis is left behind when all the others go to the pharaoh's court. She feels even worse when a falcon steals one of her precious slippers. The bird delivers the slipper to the pharaoh, who searches the kingdom until he finds Rhodopis with its mate, and makes her his queen. The parallels and differences to be seen with other Cinderella tales make this ideal for comparisons. The text is lengthy but entertainingly written.

This Western approach to ancient Egypt retains a few stylistic bits, e.g. a conventionalized lotus blossom, the rigid profile with smooth hairdo and pharaonic crown. Then there are the falcon, hippopotamus, and throne to add flavor. It appears visually more like Hollywood's ancient Egypt than *The Book of the Dead*. K or Grades 1-5.

Deborah Nourse Lattimore, **The Winged Cat: A Tale of Ancient Egypt**. HarperCollins, 1992. 32pp.
Lattimore's original story of the temple serving girl Merit's journey through the Netherworld is based on her extensive research, and includes some of the spells

and ceremonies of which we have records. Pharaoh sends Merit and Waha, the high priest, to be judged in the Netherworld, because Merit has seen the priest kill her cat but he denies it. With the cat's spirit accompanying her, Merit sets bravely forth. The priest tries to rid himself of Merit, but in the final judgment he is devoured while Merit returns to a good life. Although the text is lengthy, it is action-filled and full of information. The afterword adds much more background with enthusiasm.

Lattimore's research has rewarded us with pictures closely based on ancient Egyptian scrolls and the wall paintings from tombs. The colors are fresh and the settings those of much conventionalized Egyptian art. Figures act out the story in scenes without backgrounds, frequently with some accompanying hieroglyphics. The illustrations vary considerably in size and approach, some framed showing a sequence of action, others more decorative double-page depictions of a single event. All pages appear to be papyrus-like, for added verisimilitude. The endpapers contain an "alphabet" chart of hieroglyphics and another showing "42 City gods." Much of the hieroglyphs on the title page and elsewhere are not translated, however. Grades 1 or 2-6.

Gift of the Nile: An Egyptian Legend from the Legends of the World series retold by Jan M. Mike (Troll, 1993) tells of a slave girl who becomes the trusted counsel of the Pharaoh Senefru. There is a flavor of ancient Egypt in patterns, scarabs, dress and artifacts, the boat, and the stiffness of people's poses. Charles Reasoner's almost featureless faces and obvious contemporary page designs are serious detractions from the usefulness of this book visually.

Leontyne Price's lengthy telling of the story of *Aida* (Gulliver/HBJ, 1990), although set in Egypt, is not really an Egyptian tale. But the illustrations by Leo and Diane Dillon are worth examining for their richness of texture and skill. Small friezes atop the text pages are full of action, while the full page melodramatic operatic stage sets pictured on the opposite pages are replete with costume and architectural details from Egyptian history. The significant motifs of lotus and papyrus frame the pages and bloom on the marbleized endpapers.

Hieroglyphs from A to Z: A Rhyming Book with Ancient Egyptian Stencils for Kids (Rizzoli, 1993, co-published with the Museum of Fine Arts, Boston) illustrated by Peter Der Manuelian has rhymes for each letter of the English alphabet with the hieroglyphic symbol, where there is one, to match. More information is provided on the hieroglyphs, and on ancient Egypt as well. Stencils are included for students to write their own messages. The patterned borders and illustrations are in the Egyptian style.

For background for younger children on mummies and the beliefs about the Afterlife, Aliki's *Mummies Made in Egypt* (Harper Trophy paper, 1985) offers direct, honest reportage with line drawings and watercolors that pay homage to the Egyptian style.

David Macaulay's *Pyramid* (Houghton, 1975) contains detailed information and clear line drawings of the construction of a pyramid.

Egypt Today

Florence Parry Heide and Judith Heide Gilliland, **The Day of Ahmed's Secret**. Illustrated by Ted Lewin. Lothrop, 1990. 32pp.

Young Ahmed delivers canisters of cooking gas from his donkey cart, driving through the streets of contemporary Cairo. He meets people like the food and water vendors, hauls his heavy load up many steps, and finally is able to go home to show his family his secret accomplishment: he can write his name. Gilliland lived in Cairo for two years.

Lewin's watercolors describe Ahmed's daily life in detail. Brightness dominates each double-page scene, a sunniness that reflects off the cream-colored walls, the gray streets, the dusty automobiles, and even the white noses of loaded camels. Varying points of view show us the narrow alleys and open squares, the contrast of the modern bus and donkey cart. Everywhere are the vendors and stalls, selling everything from live rabbits to soccer balls, and the omnipresent crowds. The final scene at sundown with its deep black shadows and spot-lighted family figures seated with hands folded takes on almost religious overtones. It also reminds us of the family bunker in Beirut that Lewin has painted in the same authors' *Sami and the Time of the Troubles* (Clarion, 1992) noted below. For those who have been there, Lewin's Cairo lacks only the noise and smells to be a complete re-creation. K or Grades 1-4.

Morocco

Frances Sales, **Ibrahim**. Illustrated by Eulalia Sariola. Translated from the Catalan by Marc Simont. Lippincott/Harper, 1989. 32pp.

In this simply told but lengthy tale of contemporary Marrakesh, young Ibrahim is learning to work in his father's marketplace stall. When his friend Hassan talks about going to live out in the open desert, Ibrahim is troubled by dreams of desert freedom. His future tending the stall seems confining. Finally, in another dream, a genie reminds him that he can carry freedom in his heart, that dreams can also set you free. As he grows old, Ibrahim tells stories in his stall about his dreams and the freedom in them.

The watercolor pictures express the sunny brightness of Morocco by the transparency of their colors and the extensive use of the white page. Borderless scenes are sufficiently detailed with the items in the market and the dreamy desert to provide a sense of place. Men wear the caps, women the headcovering, and all have the clothing of the region. Naturalistic but done with an innocent eye that sees life simply, without the clutter and dirt of reality, this story is as much about a philosophy of life as about Morocco. Grades 1 or 2-4.

Lebanon

Stories of Today

Florence Parry Heide and Judith Heide Gilliland, **Sami and the Time of the Troubles**. Illustrated by Ted Lewin. Clarion, 1992. 32pp.

Having lived in contemporary Beirut for several years, Gilliland can describe the life led by a young boy amid the eruptions of gunfire on days when it is not safe to leave his family's basement refuge. There are also days when life returns to a semblance of order. Then Sami can try to imagine what life was like before "the troubles." All hope for peace to return. We do not hear much from Beirut these days, so perhaps children like Sami are starting to live a more normal life. But we always seem to have similar stories on the TV news, from Bosnia, from Cambodia. Even without knowing the details of the conflicts, children can better understand from this story the feelings of other children caught in war.

The wrecked automobile and war-ravaged buildings of the endpapers set the dramatic scene, but the airy blue that dominates the title pages hint at a more hopeful future. Visually the narrative is told in double-page scenes that emphasize the contrasts of light and shadow. Figures are solid forms with wrinkled clothing; bomb-gutted buildings show their barren interiors through gaping windows. Most dramatic are the scenes in the grandfather's basement, the place of nighttime refuge from the shelling. A single light source creates deep black spaces and models the faces of the family members. The artist paints people as individuals with character. Grades 2-6.

Lebanese Americans

Janice Shefelman's *A Peddler's Dream* (Houghton Mifflin, 1992), illustrated by Tom Shefelman, has more text than the usual picture book. It is the fictionalized success story of a real Lebanese immigrant who started as a peddler and ends by owning his own store. When he goes back to the old country to marry, we have a chance to see the wedding procession and the village.

Persia/Iran

Christopher Manson, **A Gift for the King: A Persian Tale**. Henry Holt, 1989. 32pp.

In his author's note, Manson gives the source of the story as a tale from a 16th-century collection, which in turn comes from 3rd century Rome. Artaxerxes was a real king of Persia in the 5th century B.C. who surely received lavish gifts from all over his empire. Here he takes no pleasure from any of them. Walking out quite far one day, he becomes thirsty, but nowhere in all the trappings around him is there anything to drink. When a poor shepherd boy offers him a plain old water jar, the king is so appreciative that he gives the boy all the gifts he has just received. The lengthy text has a touch of humor.

The Persians of the 5th century B.C. created buildings decorated with carvings, ceramic murals, and statues that have lasted and appear in museums today. These artifacts and other more mundane objects have been used as models for the illustrations that fill three-quarters of each double-page spread. Each is jam-packed with the minions who serve the king and with the trappings of royalty: carpets, jewels, armed soldiers, camels, chariots, and even a few discretely dressed dancing girls. A nervous line creates the forms and such embellishments as the king's curls and the camels' shagginess. Watercolors add volume and details of patterns in what appear to be colors muted or faded by time, approaching a neutral tan. Naturalistic figures assume exaggerated poses to enhance the light-heartedness of the story. Compare these illustrations with those by Zeman for Gilgamesh below. Grades 2-4.

Mats Rehnman, **The Clay Flute**. Translated by Eric Bibb. R&S Books, 1989.

No source is given but Persian miniatures inspired this story originally published in Sweden. The text is simple; unfortunately it is printed in a small, unattractive type face, so it may have to be read aloud to younger children. In an unspecified setting, Abeli the musician's son sets out with only a clay flute to seek his fortune. He encounters and angers the desert witch, who takes his flute, breaks it, and turns him into a monkey. Only the kiss of a girl who shines like the stars can change him back. Abeli is bought and sold by a jester, a singer, and finally by the Caliph for his daughter. But he plays only sad music. When the music brings disaster at the daughter's wedding, the monkey is chased into the desert where he finds the flute. In the camp of a Bedouin he finally meets a girl so moved by his playing that she kisses him and breaks the spell.

The illustrations mix full page framed scenes with large vignettes and one double-page of frenetic activity showing the Caliph's reaction to the turbulent sky and lashing waves of the catastrophe Abeli causes. Stylistically influenced by the long tradition of illustrated adventures that evolved in cultures of the Persian, Indian, and contiguous empires, many small figures crowd scenes flooded with patterns of flowers, clothes, rugs, even birds in flight. The endpapers exhibit the glory of such patterns in a rug-like spread incorporating geometric shapes with vine and flower forms printed in intense reds and blues. Grades 2-6.

Diane Stanley, **Fortune**. Morrow, 1990. 32pp.

"Long ago, in the poorest corner of Persia," Omar is too poor to marry his betrothed, Sunny, so he goes off to the market town to seek his fortune. A dancing tiger aptly named Fortune is what he finds in this original story. Fortune makes him rich, too rich for Sunny. So he seeks a suitable princess. He finds one weeping for her lost love, who magically turns out to be the tiger. Omar is again rewarded, but this time he returns to Sunny anyway, for a satisfying ending to this tartly told tale.

Stanley did her research to present us with full pages and vignettes plus border decorations in a style straight from the illustrated manuscripts and miniatures of the 16th and 17th centuries in Persia. Patterns, patterns everywhere: geometric, floral, arabesques on walls, clothing, floors, jewelry, with as glorious a rendering of a pair of peacocks as seen anywhere. Some scenes are full page with multiple borders of marbleized papers. Others are borderless ovals. All depict aspects of a place and time through artifacts, costumes, and architecture in the flat perspective characteristic of traditional Persian miniatures. Grades 1-5.

Ludmila Zeman, **Gilgamesh the King**. Tundra, 1992. 22pp.

Gilgamesh, cruel ruler of ancient Mesopotamia, was part god and part man. To answer the people's cry for help, the Sun God created Enkidu to challenge Gilgamesh, but first to live with the animals and learn compassion. With beautiful Shamhat, who came from the city to sing to him and became his love, Enkidu approaches the city walls to challenge Gilgamesh. After a terrible battle, Gilgamesh slips and begins to fall, but Enkidu saves him and becomes his friend. Peace and celebration follow. Notes on both the original story and the historical background are included.

Qualities of myth and humanistic spirituality characterize this ancient tale; both are inherent in the visual narrative as well. Horizontal layouts suggest the friezes on Babylonian walls. Suggestions of the relief carvings on these walls, mostly decorative motifs, are used to frame each illustration. The architectural settings and artifacts are of the period as well, while the landscape is properly palm-treed. Zeman uses what looks like a scratchboard medium to create illustrations that seem lit from behind. The black lines used mainly for texture, like those in hair, leafy masses, stony surfaces, are scratchy but the colors that shine through are smoothly applied pastel hues heavy on the yellows and oranges. The endpapers offer a map of the eastern Mediterranean that glows with the hot Mesopotamian sun. Animals and humans are naturalistic but somewhat simplified with faces based on the ancient sculptures that emphasize round eyes. The action is visualized in Western style, offering a good-natured version of what could be a bloody battle. Grades 2-6.

Note: Tundra is publishing Zeman's *The Revenge of Ishtar: Gilgamesh the King: Book II* in September 1993.

Susi Bohdal's *The Magic Honey Jar* (North-South, 1987), translated by Anthea Bell, uses a long text about a boy with the flu, whose dreams take him from a reading of the *Arabian Nights* to living them, as a vehicle for her interpretation of the style of the Persian miniatures. Her scenes depict architecture and costumes from some Middle Eastern time and place. She uses a variety of sizes, series of small pictures to show action, and larger illustrations to allow for groups of figures. Her style is interesting to compare with Diane Stanley's in *Fortune*, noted above.

For another variation on this style, see Safaya Salter's illustrations for *Aesop's Fables*, retold by Anne Gatti (Gulliver/Harcourt Brace, 1992).

Bedouin Life

Sue Alexander, **Nadia the Willful**. Illustrated by Lloyd Bloom. Pantheon, 1983. 48pp.

Nadia is not the usual obedient Bedouin daughter. When her favorite brother dies, her father in his grief forbids anyone to mention Hamed's name. Nadia cannot ease the pain within her without talking about Hamed, sharing her memories with the others who knew him, defying her father. Finally she persuades her father that Hamed can live on in their hearts as they talk about and remember him.

Both the soft gray pencil drawings and the thick frames around each picture, including the title page, set the stage for this mythic tale of spiritual regeneration. All figures and objects are treated the same way, as if the pencil were clay to be modelled. Draped clothes and swirling sands are blended with milling sheep and even firelight to create pictures that describe desert life as a series of harmonious events. Human gestures are dramatic, expressing clearly the anger, pain, sorrow, and compassion of each character in the tale as much about dealing with grief as about Bedouin life. Grades 2 or 3-6.

From *Nadia the Willful* by Sue Alexander. Illustrated by Lloyd Bloom. Copyright 1983. Reprinted with permission of Pantheon.

Jan Reynolds, **Sahara: Vanishing Cultures**. Harcourt Brace, 1991. 32pp.

The author's aim is to give us a picture of Tuareg life on the desert before it vanishes. She does so by going through the activities of daily life seen through the eyes of Manda, a young boy. Clear color photographs of people, plus some of the landscape, share the pages with the text. Additional details are given in author notes. The philosophy stated is one of hope: "We really are all alike no matter where we live." Grades 1 or 2-5.

Israel and Palestine

Laurie Dolphin, **Neve Shalom/Wahat al-Salam: Oasis of Peace**. Photographed by Ben Dolphin. Scholastic, 1993. 48pp.

This is not really a picture book. It is the factual story of two boys, one Jewish and one Moslem, who meet in a unique Israeli school in an experimental Arab-Jewish community. Neve Shalom/Wahat Al-Salim has opened its school to outsiders in an effort to promote harmony in this deeply troubled area. First we meet the boys and their families, both living near each other in the same country with many things in common, but with profound differences as well: they don't even speak the same language. As we watch the boys become friends, we share the hope of the author and of the founders of the "oasis." Grades 2-6.

Background Book
Another in Rizzoli's series Treasures of Asia, *Persian Painting* (1977), text by Basil Gray, gives examples of the painting that has inspired the picture book artists. Many books on Egyptian art and several on Mesopotamian art are in most libraries.

Notes

Section 5
Central and Southern Africa and African Americans

African Americans are the only minority group whose peoples were, for the most part, brought to this country against their will. The relationship between African Americans and other Americans has had a long and bitter history, punctuated by the obvious brutalities of the slavery system and by the more subtle cruelties and indignities of segregation. In light of this history, it should be no surprise to find that sensibilities are easily bruised. Both African-American children and those who are not need help to understand this sore that has been festering for so many years. If they have the opportunity to see and discuss not one or two but many books with stories about black Africa and African Americans, this need may be at least partially answered.

During the rise of the civil rights movement early in the second half of this century, books and picture books about Africa and the African American experience began to emerge in discernible numbers. Some of the best of these are still in print. Then interest in such publications seemed to fade. Recently the number of such books is again rising. From these we have tried to select the best of what we have found and examined.

Africa is a large continent. The countries into which it has been arbitrarily divided bear no necessary relationship to the many cultural groups or societies that have flourished there, and from which so many African Americans have descended. The variety of arts, crafts, and stories matches that of the cultures from which they come. We will name these when they can be specified. But for students to begin to appreciate the variety and complexity of this area, they must first see the maps, including both typographical features and group locations. Then they must realize how this heritage was changed by the conditions met by the African Americans when they came to the U.S.

All of Africa is also undergoing turmoil as its countries seek to define themselves after the period of colonial exploitation. Young children can only begin, with help, to see the complexities of the problems faced by these emerging nations. At least the names and peoples may seem a bit less strange when they have met them in the pages of picture books.

Original Tales and Folk Tales Evoking the African Past

Verna Aardema, **Bringing the Rain to Kapiti Plain: A Nandi Tale**. Illustrated by Beatriz Vidal. Dial, 1981, Pied Piper paper, 1983. 32pp.

___, **Traveling to Tondo: A Tale of the Nkundo of Zaire**. Illustrated by Will Hillenbrand. Knopf, 1991. 36pp.

___, **Who's in Rabbit's House? A Masai Tale**. Illustrated by Leo and Diane Dillon. Dial, 1977, Pied Piper paper, 1979. 32pp.

___, **Why Mosquitoes Buzz in People's Ears: A West African Tale**.
Illustrated by Leo and Diane Dillon. Dial, 1975, Pied Piper paper, 1978. 32pp.
(Caldecott Award winner.)

The reteller of many African folk tales which have been illustrated by different artists, Aardema writes simply, with a rhythm and repetition that works well for reading aloud. The above are just a few of her stories with outstanding illustrations.

The Dillons use airbrushed smooth shapes for *Why Mosquitoes Buzz...*, with white line separations that give a cloisonne effect to the double-page scenes with stylized animals and careful design, not really naturalistic. For *Who's in Rabbit's House?* they use mixed media, pastels and tempera paint, to present mixed cultural influences in a boldly dramatic fashion. Details of dress, jewelry and buildings are properly Masai, but masks and events of the play performed are Western, with exaggerated actions filling the outdoor "stage" on which the story is dramatized.

Hillenbrand represents the forested environment in tones of greens and warm browns, using just enough black drawing to define plant fronds and key characters. Light simply oozes from everywhere. The animals are depicted naturalistically but also with distinct personalities. Small silhouettes of the animals are a neat touch on some text pages. Varying viewpoints add to the pacing of the story. The endpaper design shows the African influence.

Vidal's long, horizontal double-page scenes give us a sense of the sweep of the Kenyan plains. Flat, gouache-painted shapes, frequently outlined in white, depict local birds and animals, the grasses, and changing skies with an innocence and obvious delight in composition. With Aardema's repetition of verses, Vidal has each scene add attractive fresh visual material.

Blaise Cendrars, **Shadow**. Translator and illustrator Marcia Brown. Scribners, 1982. 40pp. (Caldecott Award winner.)

Cendrars' poem is a mood piece rather than a conventional story. The Shadow that the storyteller evokes in speaking of ghosts, or ancestors, or magic, is more than a shadow; it's Shadow that we see when there is no light, that follows us but has no eyes, no voice, no shadow.

Exploiting cut papers, some of solid colors and some prepared with paints to create distant hills or walls of nearby huts, Brown describes the assorted qualities evoked in the poetic text. Double-page scenes depict the magic of this intangible reality as hunters stalk game or march off to war with spears and shields doubled by their shadows. Humans are shown in black silhouettes, naturalistic shapes sometimes against vast sweeps of plain or mountainside, sometimes around a campfire listening to a frenetic storyteller. Hints of Central Africa appear in houses, some animals, and a couple of masks. The mystic potency of the universal abstraction called "shadow" is visualized here with a sure hand and a sympathetic heart. Because there has been some objection to the "authenticity" of Shadow, this book should certainly not be used in isolation. Grades 3 or 4 up for text, younger for illustrations.

Deborah M. Newton Chocolate, reteller, **Spider and the Sky God: An Akan Legend**. Illustrated by David Albers. (Legends of the World) Troll hardback and paper, 1993. 32pp.

This *pourquoi* legend explains how Ananse the spider, who wanted to tell stories "as splendid as his webs," obtained them from the Sky God. With the help of his wife, Spider tricks and traps the Python, Hornets, Leopard, and Fairy that the Sky God demands in payment for the stories.

Strong legends such as those from West Africa dealing with this tricky spider deserve strong visual settings, pictures that distill emotion and build on forms suggestive of a people's representation in their artifacts. Here wood, a material that is very frequently used there, is cut with rough, almost crude vigor to create designed pages dominated by the black printer's ink, where the cut areas are filled with a variety of bright watercolors. Abstract animal shapes vie with geometric decorations. The potency of the Sky God's red face with its radiating yellow halo is one example of the effectiveness of this woodcut-like technique of illustration. Notes on geography, history and culture are included. Grades 1 or 2-4 or 5.

___, **Talk, Talk: An Ashanti Legend**. Illustrated by David Albers. (Legends of the World) Troll hardback and paper, 1993. 32pp.

The Ashanti belief that animals and objects have a life of their own leads into this humorous story of a farmer upset by hearing talking yams, dog, tree, and stone. When he complains to a skeptical fisherman, his fish talk. The two meet a weaver, who joins in their fright when his cloth speaks. They and a fourth man run to tell the chief, who dismisses them. But then the chief's stool speaks....

Albers uses the same woodcut-like medium as in *Spider and the Sky God* noted above, here with a similar effect. There are a few more references here to local artifacts and clothing, with more scenes depicting specific events. Notes on geography, history and culture are included. Grades 1 or 2-4 or 5.

Ruby Dee, reteller, **Tower to Heaven**. Illustrated by Jennifer Bent. Holt, 1991. 32pp.

Dee has chosen a Ghanaian version of this tale told all over Africa, using simple words and sentences for the long but light-hearted text. Many years ago the people let an old woman named Yaa do all their communicating with the sky god Onyankopon. She was a poor choice, chattering on and on, knocking him down with her pestle, until he took himself far up into the sky. To communicate with him, the people try to pile all their mortars together for a tower tall enough to reach him. Yaa climbs it first, but needs one more mortar, which the people below cannot find. So there she waits, still calling to Onyankopon, while the people have given up the search.

Heavy black outlines define figures and the special objects like mortars and pestles that help tell the tale. People in the round-hutted village are shown going about mundane tasks, but Yaa is given the spotlight as she pounds and chatters away. A rather stark version of a more universal story. Grades 2-5.

Fiona French, **King of Another Country**. Scholastic, 1993. 28pp.

French's original story is set in a non specific African country. A young, drum-playing man named Ojo lives in a village near a forest. He answers "no" to any requests for help. While lost in the forest and hungry, he picks some fruit. He refuses to ask permission when told to do so by the fierce King of the Forest, who says to Ojo that he could be a king if he could only learn to say "yes" as well as "no." Entering a door, Ojo sees the people of a city waiting to call him king. He says "yes" to this. The elders warn him he must never open a certain door. All goes well until his wife wants to open it. Now when he says "yes," they are both sent from the city.

From *King of Another Country* by Fiona French. Copyright 1993. Reprinted with permission of Scholastic.

But having learned to say both "yes" and "no," Ojo returns to his village a wiser man. The story is more a general morality play than an Africa-specific one.

But the illustrations are inspired by African arts, making the book a visual tour de force with multiple variations of patterns based on dots and lines, mostly in reds, oranges and browns. Clothing, buildings, landscapes, indeed almost all things except human flesh are constructed of geometric combinations of these patterns. The double-page scenes are redolent with bright colors, with backgrounds as washes, hints of the same hues. Heavily stylized also are the poses and gestures of the people. These illustrations project a vitality and power, an exuberance that the text barely suggests. Grades 1-4.

Mary-Joan Gerson, reteller, **Why the Sky Is Far Away: A Nigerian Folktale**. Illustrated by Carla Golembe. Joy Street/Little, Brown, 1992. 32pp.

The author notes that this story is at least five hundred years old. She tells it simply but with rich detail. Once when the sky was close to the earth, people could just take pieces of it to eat when they were hungry. They had a lot of time to weave, carve, tell stories, and have festivals. But people wasted the sky-food, so the sky grew angry, warning the oba or king, to stop the wasting or lose the bounty. The people heeded until a celebration when Adese, a woman who was never satisfied, took more than she could eat. The angry sky moved out of reach, forcing people to work at growing food.

The illustrations hint at a style that emphasizes broad gestures with few details of clothing patterns and food. The artist has incorporated some of her researched Nigerian motifs and patterns. Figures are solid black with white lines scratched into the surface to form features. Text pages have thick painted borders which, along with the endpapers, include more motifs. Bright pictures depict the simpler life before the sky left. Grades 1 or 2-5.

Barbara Knutson, reteller, **How the Guinea Fowl Got Her Spots: A Swahili Tale of Friendship**. Carolrhoda, 1990. 32pp.

From *How the Guinea Fowl Got Her Spots: A Swahili Tale of Friendship* by Barbara Knutson. Copyright 1990. Reprinted with permission of Carolrhoda.

Knutson, who was born and has lived in Africa, retells this *pourquoi* tale of a natural phenomenon. After Nganga the Guinea Fowl has saved her friend Cow twice from the hungry lion, Cow cleverly speckles the previously black fowl to help her escape the lion.

Realistic creatures in believable but minimal grass, rocks, or water are placed on wide expanses of white paper. Knutson uses black ink and watercolors on scratchboard, so that although the illustrations do not look typically African, the technique mimics some traditional Swahili designs seen incised on many utensils from that culture. This is seen clearly on the vertical designs placed under the bold black initial letters on the left side of most pages. There is a rough-and-ready quality to both the scratchboard black lines and the applied transparent paints that animates the narrative and reinforces the primal thrust of this creation story devoid of humans. K or Grades 1-4.

___, **Why the Crab Has No Head**. Carolrhoda hardback and paper, 1987. 24pp.

This *pourquoi* tale from the Bakongo people of Zaire is told in a lively fashion. After Nzambi Mpungo, creator of earth and sky, had spent all day on the elephant, she is too tired to finish Crab's head, so puts off the completion until the next day. Crab proudly invites all the other animals to come see how magnificent he will be since it has taken so long to complete him. Hearing the fuss, Nzambi decides Crab is fine without a head. This embarrasses Crab so much that he no longer walks so proudly.

A simply told tale can retain its significance if it is simply visualized. Here a smoothly applied black contrasts with the off-white of the small pages to create bordered pictures and blocks of text. Each border is unique, sometimes housing geometric patterns and sometimes including representations of animals relating to the text. Looking like linoleum cuts, the illustrations emphasize the decorative possibilities of feathers, scales, vegetation, reminiscent of those in some African textiles and carvings. The multiple patterns on the rooster and the sensual swaying of the river grasses are particularly imaginative examples. Within the surface simplicity there is a complexity of design pointing to more complex readings of the story. Grades 1-4.

Eric Maddern, reteller, **The Fire Children: A West African Creation Tale**. Illustrated by Frane Lessac. Dial, 1993, 28pp.

When Nyame, the great sky god, was admiring the Earth he had made, Aso Yaa and Kwaku Ananse, two curious spirit people, were sneezed out onto the Earth from his mouth. Feeling lonely in her cave, Aso Yaa persuades Kwaku Ananse to make and bake some little children. Each time Nyame comes to check on them they either hide the children half-baked or must leave them baking too long, so the children turn out to be of many colors. When life is breathed into them, they play, grow, and wander all over the earth, being the differing colors people still are today.

     Endpapers picture a Garden of Eden with a river and a multitude of tropical flora and fauna. Lessac's choice of opaque gouache paint and a pseudo-childlike style are appropriate for this innocent vision of part of the creation story. The double-page scenes fill the pages with the details of paradise. The god's face is based on a West African mask, while pottery patterns and cave decorations also stem from that region. The spirit people are brown, the ground golden, the sky a cloud-puffed blue. The visuals all convey a strong sense of good feelings enhanced by the story of the children of many colors all loved by those who made them. K or Grades 1-4.

Francesca Martin, reteller, **The Honey Hunters: A Traditional African Tale**. Candlewick, 1992. 28pp.

Kenyan-born Martin has adapted, in rhythmic prose, a traditional tale told by the Ngoni people of Africa. Long ago all the animals were friends, and all loved honey. A little gray bird called the honey guide knew how to find it, and would call "follow me." One day a boy is followed by a rooster, then a bush cat, an antelope, a leopard, a zebra, a lion, and finally an elephant to the tree the bird shows them. The boy gives out pieces of the honeycomb to be shared. But the animals fight instead, and can never be friends again. Yet still the honey guide calls "Che che!..."

     There seems to be irony in setting this sad tale of universal greed into double-page scenes of delicacy and peace within multiple borders. Watercolored with an eye for both the decorative and the realistic, with minute details of feather and fur, of various trees in full blossom, all is composed in scenes of jungle and plains. Sequences of vignettes are used inventively to show animals added and falling out of the action. K or Grades 1-4.

Gerald McDermott, **Zomo the Rabbit: A Trickster Tale from West Africa**. Harcourt Brace, 1992. 32pp.

Zomo the trickster rabbit of West African oral tradition jauntily hops through this humorous tale. Although he is clever, Zomo also wants wisdom, a distinction which may be difficult for children to discern. Asking Sky God to give him wisdom, Zomo is given three seemingly impossible tasks. He uses his cleverness in amusing and successful encounters with Big Fish, Wild Cow and Leopard, only to receive some sly wisdom in return.

     Influenced by western African designs, the figures and objects here have been filtered through the artist's interpretive biases that tend to exploit geometric shapes for most things: the decorations on Zomo's jacket, Sky God's facial features, Big Fish's fins and scales, even the hill's floral landscape. Sharp edges create stencil-like shapes. Saturated gouache pigments produce intensely colored double-page scenes heavy in the yellows. The boldness of the paintings match the braveness of the rabbit's behavior. K-Grade 3.

Tololwa M. Mollel, **The King and the Tortoise**. Illustrated by Kathy Blankley. Clarion, 1993. 32pp.

In this sprightly retelling of a story from Cameroon, a king challenges all creatures to prove that they are smarter than he is by making him a robe out of smoke. First the hare brags, tries, and fails, as do the fox, leopard and elephant. Then comes the tortoise, who asks seven days' time, plus the king must promise to give him whatever materials he needs for the job. When the week has passed, tortoise says he just needs more thread to finish. To fulfill his promise, the king must give him "thread of fire" to finish a robe of smoke. The king has to admit the tortoise is as clever as he is.

The double-page scenes here are enlivened by a variety of decorative borders, using geometric devices like those on the endpapers. Pastels produce a textured yellowish surface while they create naturalistic animals and humans in appropriate clothes. Black outlines help define the range of gestures in response to the smoky activities as the competing animals gyrate in the swirling clouds of purplish-white vapors. The text is unobtrusively integrated into these scenes, which are composed to focus on the sequenced trials. Turtle and king are particularly individualistic; the king's ornately colorful throne is simply splendid. Grades 2-4 or 5.

___, **The Orphan Boy: A Masai Story**. Illustrated by Paul Morin. Clarion, 1990.

This long, descriptive *pourquoi* story from the author's homeland tells of Kileken, the orphan boy who becomes an old man's helper and companion the same night a familiar star is missing in the sky. The boy accomplishes amazing deeds, somehow feeding and watering the cattle in a drought, but claims he cannot tell the secret of how he does it. The old man follows him to see his magic, but in losing his trust he loses the boy, who becomes the planet Venus, called Kileken, the orphan boy, because it rises at dawn and returns at nightfall.

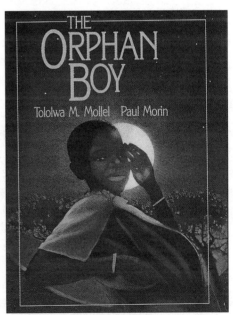

From *The Orphan Boy* by Tololwa M. Mollel. Illustrated by Paul Morin. Copyright 1990. Reprinted with permission of Clarion.

Finely crafted and fully detailed paintings convince us of the parching drought in tones of yellowish browns, then bring alive the miracle of Kileken's power in a spotlighted radiant blue sky. The paintings, full-page or across most of a double-page spread, incorporate textures to enhance areas of landscape, walls, and fabric like the old man's red mantle. Morin infuses his naturalism with a spiritual quality encompassing human imperfection as well as hope. Grades 2-5.

___, **A Promise to the Sun: An African Story**. Illustrated by Beatriz Vidal. Little, Brown, 1992. 32pp.

The Masai-born author has here invented his own *pourquoi* tale with African background to explain why bats fly only at night. Long ago during a terrible drought in the land of the birds, the bat was chosen to seek rain. He is sent by Moon to Stars to Clouds to Winds, finally to the Sun, who agrees to help only if bat and the others will build him a nest in the forest to rest in at the end of the day. But the birds will not honor the agreement. The Sun keeps bringing clouds and rain, hoping for its nest. Ashamed, bats have hidden from the sun ever since.

The format of wide double-page spreads and mixed media illustrations is similar to others by Vidal, like *The Legend of El Dorado* (Knopf, 1991) noted later. Here the rendering of the many birds is naturalistic; from parrot to peacock we are treated to a display of ornithological splendor. The landscape and vegetation are more abstractly handled. The elements are imagined in effectively expressive ways: the winds swirl in multicolored spirals, the sun's flaming hairdo leaves burning locks in its wake. The birds themselves seem to find ways of flying or roosting in decorative relationships. The openness of the layout allows the straightforward text to find comfortable places to roost. Grades 2-5.

___, **The Princess Who Lost Her Hair: An Akamba Legend**. Illustrated by Charles Reasoner. (Legends of the World) Troll hardback and paper, 1993. 32pp.

Another sprightly although lengthy retelling by this Africa-born author concerns a lovely princess, too vain about her beautiful long hair to spare even a bit for a passing bird. The bird warns her that a coming drought will cause both the leaves and her hair to fall, and so it does. Muoma the beggar boy has seen in his dreams a way to restore what was lost. On his quest, he is generous, and in turn teaches the princess to be as well. Of course, all ends happily.

There is a kind of airbrushed smoothness to the illustrations that denies the drama of this Kenyan tale. Use of regional patterns on clothes adds a touch of geographic specificity. But the expressionless faces and slick Western design give a saccharine taste to a tender tale. The author is not well served by his illustrator here. As in the rest of this series, a map and notes about the area and culture relating to the story are helpful. Grades 2-4.

Judy Sierra, **The Elephant's Wrestling Match**. Illustrated by Brian Pinkney. Dutton/Lodestar, 1992. 32pp.

In this simple retelling of a folk tale from Cameroon, the elephant challenges any of the animals to wrestle with him, with monkey sending the message on a talking drum. One by one the leopard, the crocodile, the rhinoceros are overcome. Then the tiny bat arrives, and, getting inside his ear, brings elephant to the ground. The angry elephant smashes the drum, so monkeys can no longer beat it. The text has humor, rhythm and repetition. A note gives more information on the talking drum and on the source of the story.

Pinkney's illustrations are large pictures of the animals in the story, all native to central Africa, plus hints of the typical landscape. His scratchboard technique enhances modeling of the naturalistic three-dimensional forms set against a wispy blue-painted sky. K-Grades 4.

John Steptoe, **Mufaro's Beautiful Daughters: An African Tale**. Lothrop, 1987. 32pp.

Inspired by a folk tale collected from near the ruins of a once important city in Zimbabwe, this story includes elements familiar from European fairy tales. One beautiful daughter, Nyasha, is as good as she is lovely, but her sister Manyara is vain and selfish. When the king invites the daughters of the land to come to his city so that he can choose a wife, Manyara pushes herself ahead and reveals her true character. Nyasha takes the time to be kind and considerate, and so is chosen to be queen.

Steptoe creates a lush and vibrant community, the jungle verdant, the blossoms exotic, the birds technicolor. The city is splendidly built on stone terraces with sculptures and patterned inlays. On the double-page spreads are real people, each perceived in portraits that express individual personality. The lengthy text is integrated into spaces left open for it. Forms are developed using fine cross-hatching and limited paint. This grandly romantic presentation of another time and place won a Caldecott award. Grades 1 or 2-5.

Veronique Tadjo, **Lord of the Dance: An African Retelling**. Lippincott, 1988. 28pp.

The Ivory Coast born author has adapted Sidney Carter's English hymn to relate to Senufo ceremony and custom. From the earth's beginning, as her poetic song goes, the Mask was there to lead the dances as was the Lord of the Dance in the original hymn. Although the images carved of him have been put away as city life developed, the Mask endures as the spirit of nature and of the ancestors. Notes offer a map and describe the Senufo people and the significance of the masks.

In the spirit of the brown vegetable ink drawings of the Senufo, drawings of people and animals that share some qualities with those of the Australian aboriginals, Tadjo has created full-color pictures. Some are based on carved wooden masks, some are framed with decorative borders, some depict people, others are simply massed symbols. These illustrations, isolated elements of which occupy the endpapers, are highly abstract and are expressive of the magic of the mask and its role in the life of many Africans. Grades 2-5 or 6.

David Wisniewski, **Sundiata: Lion King of Mali**. Clarion, 1992. 32pp.

This tale from the oral tradition of the griots, or storytellers, has a basis in the facts we know about the king of Mali and 13th-century Africa. Sundiata does not speak or walk as a child, so when his father dies the crown goes to a step-brother, the child of a rival wife of the king. The prince and his mother go into exile, while the adviser given Sundiata by his father is sent to the court of the wicked sorcerer Sumanguru. When Sumanguru begins to conquer all the land, Sundiata defeats him in an exciting battle, saves his people, and rules them "for many golden years." Although lengthy, the story is rich in detail and adventure. Wisniewski's extensive notes detail historic fact and accuracy of illustration along with technique used.

From *Sundiata: Lion King of Mali* by David Wisniewski. Copyright 1992. Reprinted with permission of Clarion.

His unique approach to cut paper, using multiple razor-cut layers photographed for the effects of light and shadow, is a fine foil for the mythic qualities of a hero's story. Using designs and artifacts adapted from several west African groups, and brilliant colors, he creates double-page scenes as stage sets in which the characters play out their roles with dramatic effectiveness. Mantles swirl as riders charge; intricately cut dust clouds add a sense of urgency to an army's movements. The text appears in superimposed, elaborately framed white boxes, which unfortunately detract from the strong emotional impact of the imaginatively conceived layouts. Grades 2 or 3-6.

In the warrior tradition of Sundiata is Diane Stanley and Peter Vennema's *Shaka, King of the Zulus* (Morrow, 1988) with illustrations by Stanley that emphasize local details of clothing, buildings, landscape, artifacts, and beaded designs for borders. This biography in picture book format describes the life of this mighty warrior of the early 19th century.

For brief introductions to some of the customs of 26 African cultures see Margaret Musgrove's *Ashanti to Zulu: African Traditions* (Dial, 1976, Puffin paper, 1980) with the carefully researched, Caldecott-winning illustrations by Leo and Diane Dillon.

There are many collections of African folk tales available. Among them are several by Ashley Bryan, a fine storyteller, including *Beat the Story Drum, Pum-Pum* (Atheneum, 1980) illustrated by him with his distinctive decorative, almost woodcut-like solid forms.

Contemporary Central and Southern Africa

Lloyd Alexander, **The Fortune-Tellers**. Illustrated by Trina Schart Hyman. Dutton, 1992. 32pp.

Alexander's original, richly told adventure story has the quality of legend, although not set in ancient or mythical times. A young man, not content with his life, seeks to learn his future from an old fortune-teller. The predictions will be obviously silly and self-evident to the audience, but the young man believes and acts upon them. A series of wild, humorous and romantic adventures follows, ending in success for the hero.

Though timeless in concept, Hyman has set the tale in a town in contemporary Cameroon, complete with bars, oxcarts on the unpaved main street, and stalls selling the stuff of mundane living. Her paintings in mixed media create an environment that one can almost hear and smell. The double-page scenes are rich with the wonderfully varied colors and patterns of local dress, the details of shops, pottery, carvings, even the goats, monkeys and lizards that coexist with the individually portrayed characters. The pictures are designed to accept the many lines of text comfortably. Each scene shows a community busy about its work, enjoying it in a good-natured way. The influence of her visit to Cameroon is obvious in the joy and humor Hyman brings to these wonderfully alive illustrations. Grades 1-5.

Joy Anderson, **Juma and the Magic Jinn**. Illustrated by Charles Mikolaycak. Lothrop, 1986. 32pp.

This is not a legend or a folk tale, although it has a magical quality, but was inspired by a visit to the island of Lamu off the coast of Kenya. Juma, a young boy, is sent home from school for his attention to picture-drawing and poetry-writing instead of arithmetic. Warned against the jinn jar by his mother and his friends, the men at Omar's Tea Shop, Juma nevertheless calls his own jinn from the jar. The requests he makes are predictably unsatisfying, until he makes the one that brings him home again with new appreciation. Although long, the story is simply told. The moral is obvious but not overdone, implicit in the story replete with names, some words, and background of life on Lamu.

Mikolaycak's illustrations do not attempt to imitate any African or Kenyan style. His images are quite realistic depictions of the people, costume, buildings and scenery of the island, including the Islamic traditions. The border design he runs along the bottom of the wordy pages of text helps maintain the exotic atmosphere created by the patterns found on the fabrics and furniture in the full-page scenes of Juma's village and of his magical adventures. Juma's dark skin may suggest Africa, but there is a sense of the Middle East or North Africa, perhaps because this is a Muslim community. Grades 1 or 2-4.

Sonia Appiah, **Amoko and Efua Bear**. Illustrated by Carol Easmon. Macmillan, 1988. 32pp.

This simple but wordy story of a small girl's life with her family, friends, and her special toy bear could be set anywhere. Perhaps because both author and illustrator have Ghanaian connections, the story takes place in Ghana today. Amoko accidently leaves her special bear outside, but he is found and fixed for her.

There's a folk art-like stiffness to this series of full-page paintings. Things and people seem isolated in space, painted with flat, opaque, unmodulated surfaces. Amoko and her father stand behind a table in an almost empty room, the table holding cut-out-looking vegetables and meat, while through a window two palm trees stand against a pale blue sky. The costumes and scenery evoke Africa in this simplistic picture of village life. K-Grade 2.

Hannah Heritage Bozylinsky, **Lala Salama: An African Lullaby in Swahili and English**. Philomel, 1993. 32pp.

The text simply tells all the animals to sleep well, in peace, along with the mother and child. The author's note adds information on Masai life and customs gathered from her personal visit.

Double-page scenes with a thin white border are set on tan pages, with borders frequently broken by the black-outlined figures and objects. Mother and son have bald heads and wear appropriate dress and jewelry. They live in a typical round house. The pictures are naturalistic but are designed more for their attractive layout than natural history. The unmodelled surfaces tend to be conventionalized. The inclusion of local trees, flowers, and grasses adds to the attractiveness. The five to ten words per scene are at ease in the overall layout of this peaceful book. K-Grade 2.

Jane Cowen-Fletcher, **It Takes a Village**. Scholastic, 1993. 32pp.

Yemi is proud to be left in charge of her little brother "all by herself" when her mama goes to sell mangoes in the market. When Kokou wanders off, Yemi worries that he will be hungry, thirsty, frightened, hot, and tired. She soon learns the truth of the African proverb "It takes a village to raise a child" as she finds all the people of the village who have taken care to see that Kokou is fine. She thanks them all, in this simply but effectively written picture of life in a rural Benin village. The author adds a note on the traditional markets and items shown.

From *It Takes a Village* by Jane Cowen-Fletcher. Copyright 1993. Reprinted with permission of Scholastic.

The book's message is clearly pictured in a sequence of scenes that juxtapose each of Yeni's concerns with a villager's caring solution: Kokou's hunger is assuaged by the rice vendor, his fatigue by a nap on a mat-vendor's floor, and so forth. Realistic, simplified, black-outlined figures with transparent colors against white backgrounds focus attention on the local objects and decorated fabrics. K-Grade 4.

Niki Daly, **Not So Fast, Songololo**. Atheneum/Margaret K. McElderry, 1986, Pied Piper paper, 1987. 32pp.

Young Malusi helps his granny Gogo go shopping in a city in South Africa. They ride the bus and look in the shop windows. After Gogo finishes shopping, they stop at a store where Malusi had admired new red and white tackies, or sneakers. His old ones had holes. Fortunately Gogo has enough money to buy him new ones. With these he walks so happily and proudly that his granny has to call out the title, using her pet name for him, so she can keep up with him.

Watercolors, well-diluted and applied more to suggest qualities of things than to define them, do a convincing job of creating real people and a sense of a particular place. Half-title and title pages introduce a loving grandmother and active grandson. The double-page illustrations use the whiteness of the pages for the simple text but also to focus our attentions on the adventures of the protagonists. Their symbiotic relationship is shown as much in their mutual glances as in the demonstrations of respectful help. K-Grades 3.

Ann Grifalconi, **Flyaway Girl**. Little, Brown, 1992. 32pp.

Grifalconi has incorporated an African chant into her rather long and detailed story of a young girl's coming of age. Carefree Nsia is always flying here and there, until her mother gives her the responsibility of gathering the rushes from the banks of the Niger for New Year's baskets. Nsia learns to slow down and listen, as the spirits help her find what she seeks.

Modified photographs are used as collage elements to express the spiritual quality of Nsia's life. Some of the full-page pictures opposite the pages of text illustrate specific activities, like people doing field work, while others are more metaphoric, like the superimposition of pictures of masks as Nsia walks in the river. Collectively the images of rural life along the Niger provide specifics of dress and behavior. More abstractly, they help us sense the quality of life. The decorative designs on the white pages with the text add more African texture. Grades 1 or 2-4.

Grifalconi has also produced three books about life in an African village in the jungle: *The Village of Round and Square Houses* (Little, Brown, 1986), a Caldecott Honor Book, which is specifically based on her experience in Cameroon; *Darkness and the Butterfly* (Little, Brown, 1987), and *Osa's Pride* (Little, Brown, 1990) both about a young girl and her life with her family in a less specific jungle village. All three books are illustrated realistically in full-page, full color pastels, showing houses, landscape, and people in appropriate costume.

Rachel Isadora, **Over the Green Hills**. Greenwillow, 1992. 32pp.

Young Zolani and his mother go from their hut in the Transkei, a rural black homeland in South Africa near the ocean, to visit Grandma Zindzi. They pass the village, and other travellers, picking up items to bring grandma. As they go through green fields, Zolani remembers the drought, when grandma had to live with them. When they arrive at her house, grandma has gone visiting. They are about to leave when she comes home for a happy reunion. A warm family story, told in simple text, with a few notes of clarification from the author.

Double-page watercolor paintings describe an attractive land and seascape, lush vegetation, bright whitewashed buildings, and people tending to routine chores, people with personality and a solid sense of humanity. The paints build forms rather loosely, giving an organic vitality to earth, pigs, and sky as well as the people. K-Grade 3.

Hugh Lewin, **Jafta**. Illustrated by Lisa Kopper. Carolrhoda paper, 1983. 24pp.

___, **Jafta and the Wedding**. Illustrated by Lisa Kopper. Carolrhoda paper, 1983. 24pp.

___, **Jafta—The Journey**. Illustrated by Lisa Kopper. Carolrhoda paper, 1984. 24pp.

___, **Jafta—The Town**. Illustrated by Lisa Kopper. Carolrhoda paper, 1984. 24pp.

___, **Jafta's Father**. Illustrated by Lisa Kopper. Carolrhoda paper, 1983. 24pp.

___, **Jafta's Mother**. Illustrated by Lisa Kopper. Carolrhoda hardback and paper, 1983. 24pp.

Lewin, who was born in South Africa, wrote this series about the life of a black child to introduce that life to his own children now living with him in England. Jafta is modelled on several individuals, and has no special cultural background. He seems very real in each of these simple, almost poetic stories, which are matter-of-fact about life under apartheid, and the joys of family life despite the difficulties such as fathers having to live separate from their families.

From *Jafta* by High Lewin. Illustrated by Lisa Kopper. Copyright 1983. Reprinted with permission of Carolrhoda.

Kopper's naturalistic sepia-brown wash drawings people the pages with Jafta, his family and friends, amid scenes of the countryside and the crowded city. K-Grades 3 or 4.

Ingrid Mennen and Niki Daly, **Somewhere in Africa**. Illustrated by Nicolaas Maritz. Dutton, 1990. 32pp.

The simple text reminds the reader that although there are still wild animals in Africa, boys like Ashraf live in large cities where there are tall buildings, heavy traffic, and merchants along with dancers and drummers at the supermarket. The sun is hot, but the library is cool. Ashraf's favorite book is about the wild animals that share his continent, animals that he has never seen.

We walk with Ashraf through the city as the artist uses thickly applied paints to depict his almost crudely rendered environment. Maritz offers us impressionistic views of a city like Capetown, one that our hero seems to thrive in. The thin black line-framed lively paintings frequently use the brief text as captions. K-Grade 4.

Sanna Stanley, **The Rains Are Coming**. Greenwillow, 1993. 24pp.

In this simple story of a little girl's birthday, the author has used her experience to depict life in a village in Zaire. As Aimee, a missionary's daughter, goes to collect her friends from their tasks for her party, the rain clouds gather. Her father arrives home as they all go inside for the party when the rain begins.

Aqua tints produce hazy images and, in this case, tints of color. The results are double-page scenes of a small village going about its business as the people prepare for the approaching storm. As the skies darken and the wind picks up, the pace quickens; even the chickens hustle into their shed. Aimee is shown as the only white child; all her friends in the village are African. The author notes the setting and other items of interest. K-Grades 2.

Dianne Stewart, **The Dove**. Illustrated by Jude Daly. Greenwillow, 1993. 32pp.

After a great flood in the Valley of a Thousand Hills near Durban, South Africa, Lindi and her grandmother must take their beadwork to sell in the city. Times are hard, and grandmother is worried. Inspired by the dove that had come after the rain, like the one in the Bible after the Flood, Lindi asks her grandmother to help her make a stuffed and beaded bird. Of all the beadwork they have made, the dove is the item the craft shop buys, a sign of hope for their future. Both the author and the illustrator live in South Africa.

The simple clarity of objects and somewhat distorted proportions of the people and landscape suggest folk art, like the beadwork in the story. Varied sizes of rectangular scenes in sequence add a special character to the event-filled prose. The artist paints the interior of a train with seated and standing riders and pieces of luggage on the racks. Patterns on clothing are given minute attention. The directness of the picture-making is appropriate for the loving nature of the telling. K-Grade 3.

Catherine Stock, **Armien's Fishing Trip**. Morrow, 1990. 32pp.

A note tells us that Kalk Bay in South Africa, the scene of this story, is a fishing community with some "coloured" families among its varied inhabitants. Young Armien, our hero, is Muslim. On a visit to the Bay, Armien stows away on his uncle's boat, and helps save one of the men during a storm. All ends well in this slice of life told simply but dramatically.

Stock's endpapers introduce the fishing village and surrounding sea and coastline. Her watercolors capture the bustle of the fishermen's life and the crisis of the storm. Vignettes combine with double-page scenes to present many aspects of the way of life of this community stock has visited and admired. K or Grades 1-3 or 4.

Karen Lynn Williams, **Galimoto**. Illustrated by Catherine Stock. Lothrop, 1990. 32pp.

Seven-year-old Kondi hopes to collect enough wire to build a *galimoto*, a push-toy in the shape of a vehicle, made by children in Malawi. He trades with a friend, asks various merchants, and scrounges all around his village. By nightfall he has gathered enough to form a car-shaped toy to run with along with his friends. The author gives further information on *galimoto*, the word for "car" in Chichewa, the language of Mali.

Watery watercolors that spread over the double pages paint a portrait of a village and its inhabitants, but mostly of Kondi, a creative young man with a mission. Inside a shop we see goods on shelves, outside are the food vendors with their baskets, while at home are Kondi's mother and sisters pounding maize. All around are the buildings, vegetation, and village people at work. K-Grade 3.

From the letters she wrote back to her friends in New York, eight-year-old Nila K. Leigh has produced *Learning to Swim in Swaziland: A Child's-Eye View of a Southern African Country* (Scholastic, 1993). It is printed as she printed it by hand, illustrated by her drawings plus some photographs, and refreshingly full of the sorts of information children will find fascinating, like how the stars you see are different, the English sounds strange, how babies are tied on your back, how families live....

For brief background information on different ethnic groups, their language and counting styles, see Claudia Zaslavsky's *Count on Your Fingers African Style* (Crowell, 1980) illustrated by Jerry Pinkney with realistic black and white drawings.

Background Book

Margaret Courtney-Clarke, **African Canvas**. Rizzoli, 1990. 204pp.

Although written for adults and concerned only with the art of women of West Africa, the 180 stunning color photographs give examples of architecture, pottery, body painting, fabric design and mural art reflecting the art of Africa today.

African Americans and the African Heritage

Eloise Greenfield, **Africa Dream**. Illustrated by Carole Byard. John Day, 1977. 32pp.

In a dream an African-American girl goes back to "long-ago Africa." She shops in old markets, sees strange buildings and villages. She meets her "long-ago granddaddy," relatives and friends until, as a tired baby, she is rocked to sleep by her "long-ago grandma with Mama's face," content with feeling her connection to her African heritage. The poetic text is printed on oyster-white paper.

This surface is also a fine ground for Byard's charcoal drawings, a medium particularly appropriate for picturing dreams. These double pages exploit the charcoal's ability to render the dark blacks of a starless night as well as the whispers of gray of a baby's sleeping face. Inventive imagery puts the soul into the more descriptive lines of text. K or Grades 1-4.

Virginia Kroll, **Africa: Brothers and Sisters**. Illustrated by Vanessa French. Four Winds, 1993. 32pp.

The author uses the framework of a game of question and answer between father and son to describe various African tribes and their accomplishments; these Africans are his "brothers and sisters." In addition to the businessmen, engineers, and teachers, there are dancers, musicians, artists of many kinds, farmers, and of course, storytellers. A good counter for stereotypes. The prose is direct and uncomplicated.

Framed in decorative borders suggesting fabric patterns from Africa, these watercolor double-page scenes integrate Jesse and his father briefly with some aspects of each named African group and its art: Baule masks, Falisha pottery, and Zulu baskets. Naturalistic in gesture and object definition, the illustrations are composed to demonstrate the loving relationship of father and son. Maps, a pronunciation guide, and the author's further notes on the peoples discussed are included. Grades 1 or 2-5.

___, **Masai and I**. Illustrated by Nancy Carpenter. Four Winds, 1992. 32pp.

When an African-American girl learns about the Masai people of East Africa, she feels a kinship. All during her day, after school, going to her apartment, back to school next day, preparing for a party, she continues to contrast her life with what it would be if she were a Masai girl instead. She tries to behave with what she feels would be Masai dignity and pride, while she notes the differences.

The double-page illustrations, in the main, visualize on the left the here and now world of school, dinner with the family, and chores with the vision of the Masai counterpart on the right. The scenes flow smoothly together for greater intimacy. Naturalistic oil paintings with color pencil outlines are informative, offering details like the shaved heads and beaded collars, buildings and animals, while showing the parallels between the cultures without a hierarchy of values. Grades 1-5.

Phil Mendez, **The Black Snowman**. Illustrated by Carole Byard. Scholastic, 1989. 48pp.

Introductory pages present the storyteller of West Africa, wrapped in the colorful magic Kente cloth. The arrival of slavers ends the storytelling, but not the Kente magic. In a text too lengthy for the usual picture book, Mendez tells the story of young Jacob's bitterness because of the poverty of his family at Christmas. Even the snowman he makes with his brother Peewee has to be black because of the dirt of the city. When Peewee finds a piece of Kente cloth to drape around him, the snowman comes alive. He not only challenges Jacob's denigration of black things and people but comes to him in his dreams to perform other magic and change Jacob's outlook on life.

Byard creates a sense of place, whether painting the streets of New York City or Africa, with full-page borderless pictures produced with intense colors of pastel chalks. Theatrical in their expressive suggestiveness, her illustrations use an assortment of close-ups and fuller settings. The brothers are real children with idiosyncratic personalities, but there is also a sense of drama and magic in the scenes involving the snowman and his Kente cloth. Grades 2-5.

Karen Lynn Williams, **When Africa Was Home**. Illustrated by Floyd Cooper. Orchard, 1991. 32pp.

Blond, blue-eyed Peter was born in Africa, played with African children, and was used to African ways. When told he had to go "home" to America, he was not happy. Everything is strange on arrival, especially the cold and snow. Peter and his family miss Africa, and are delighted to go back when his father finds another job there. His friends are glad to see him back. The author tells the straightforward story based perhaps on the three years spent with her family in Africa.

by Karen Lynn Williams • pictures by Floyd Cooper

WHEN AFRICA WAS HOME

From *When Africa Was Home* by Karen Lynn Williams. Illustrated by Floyd Cooper. Copyright 1991. Reprinted with permission of Orchard.

The opening double-page scene is a double portrait: the African nanny with baby Peter tied to her back so their heads touch. This visual metaphor of cultural relationship permeates the remaining scenes as we see Peter playing with his African friends, going briefly to America, and returning to continue his happy life in Africa. The paintings fill the pages with sufficient detail of local custom and landscape for us to understand its appeal. Opaque paints on a pebbled surface create fuzzy effects, at times like pastels. K-Grades 3.

Camille Yarbrough, **Cornrows**. Illustrated by Carole Byard. Putnam/ Sandcastle paper, 1992. 48pp.

While young Shirley Ann tells about her family life, she also describes her Great-Grammaw fixing her Mama's hair in braided cornrows. This is a chance for Great-Grammaw to talk about the spirit of her people, their history and culture in Africa, the terrible effect of the slave trade, the names of important African Americans, all braided together with rhythmic verses.

The sensitively modeled charcoal drawings, which have lost some luster in their reproduction on the book's double-page spreads, also picture the people and places. The story's characters, famous or simply family members, are created as individually defined humans, while several wood sculptures are rendered with respectful care. Bits and pieces of background add historical flavor. There is an overarching rhapsodic quality that suits the message of the poetic text. Grades 2-4 or 5.

African-American Folk Tales

Patricia C. McKissack, **Mirandy and Brother Wind**. Illustrated by Jerry Pinkney. Knopf, 1988. 32pp.

The author re-creates her grandparents' strutting cakewalk dance early in the century and combines it with a character called Brother Wind. In colloquial, lively prose she tells how young Mirandy aims to win the junior cakewalk contest by catching Brother Wind, scorning her clumsy friend Ezel on the way. The conjure woman helps her catch Wind, who must then do her bidding. Amid the excitement of the approaching cakewalk, she invites Ezel to be her partner. Together they seem to "dance with the wind" in this lengthy story as high-spirited as the dance itself.

Transparent watercolors create a genuine turn-of-the-century rural community with a cast of characters that seem equally real. Even the animals have personalities. Rooms show the daily activities. Pinkney manages to make Brother Wind believable, all fancied up in high hat, tie, and checkered pants, face rendered in tints of blue. Landscapes are full of the flowers and greenery of summer. The double-page scenes are filled with the details of a happy life style. Grades 2-5.

Robert D. San Souci, **Sukey and the Mermaid**. Illustrated by Brian Pinkney. Four Winds, 1992. 32pp.

The lengthy text is based on a fragmentary South Carolina folk tale, as noted by the author. A young girl who is made to work hard by her lazy stepfather takes a break on the beach and sings a song to "Mama Jo." A mermaid appears, bringing her treasures, but warns it must be a secret. However, her mother and stepfather discover it and try to catch the mermaid, who will then no longer come. Life at home becomes so bad that young Sukey decides to join the mermaid under the sea. When she pines for home, the mermaid sends her back with gold, and the name of the man she is to marry. Her stepfather steals the treasure and kills her man, but the mermaid returns to set everything straight one last time.

Some of the mythic quality of the story is expressed in the scratchboard illustrations on creamy-toned text pages. Full page and double-page scenes depict realistic characters and settings with details of dress, interiors, and the sea, enough to produce a mood of exotic anticipation. The focus is on the people and their interactions. Grades 2-6.

Brian Pinkney has also illustrated in the same style *The Ballad of Belle Dorcas* (Knopf, 1990), a short chapter book by William H. Hooks. This conjure tale from North Carolina concerns beautiful Belle, who gives up her freedom to marry a slave and uses the conjure woman's spell to save him.

___, **The Talking Eggs: A Folktale from the American South**. Illustrated by Jerry Pinkney. Dial, 1989. 32pp.

This lengthy story of two sisters, the spoiled and lazy Rose and the hard-working Blanche, has echoes in more traditional fairy tales. Blanche is kind to an old woman and is rewarded, but greedy Rose and her mother get their just deserts.

Pinkney's illustrations are similar and equally effective as in McKissack's *Mirandy and Brother Wind* (see above) Grades 2-5.

Jan Wahl, **Little Eight John**. Illustrated by Wil Clay. Lodestar/Dutton, 1992. 32pp.

In this humorous, simply told folk tale from rural North Carolina, Little Eight John is a mean kid who doesn't listen to his mother. When he kicks toads and brings bad luck, or sits backwards in his chair and brings troubles, or counts his teeth and brings sickness, he just laughs. But when he moans and groans on

Sunday, Old Raw Head Bloody Bones walks in and turns him into a spot of jam, which his mother almost washes away. Fortunately Little Eight John wakes up and promises to mind his mother, "and he always did."

Mother's admonitions are mostly pictured in small vignetted rectangles superimposed on double-page scenes of her son's mischievous actions. Other double pages show the calamities that arrive as promised. Opaque acrylic paints combine a fuzzy naturalism with occasional multiple images and even a bit of grotesque exaggeration. Little Eight John's many portraits portray the personality of an emerging teenager. K-Grade 3.

___, **Tailypo!** Illustrated by Wil Clay. Holt, 1991. 32pp.

"Way down in the big woods of Tennessee" an old man whacks the tail off a terrible creature and eats it. But the creature keeps asking for his "tailypo" back. Simply and rhythmically the tale gathers momentum as the creature persists to the scary climax.

Clay's illustrations are similar in style to those in *Little Eight John* (above) but more expressionistic with a melodramatic use of paint for this still humorous but more dramatic story. Settings at night and in firelight permit more scenes that give ghost-story goose bumps. Grades 1-4.

Joel Chandler Harris's collected *Adventures of Brer Rabbit* are important African-American folk tales that do not appear in picture books. Two sets of these have been published recently, both well-retold and both competently and imaginatively illustrated.

Julius Lester's versions are *The Tales of Uncle Remus* (1987), *More Tales of Uncle Remus* (1988), and *Further Tales of Uncle Remus* (1990), all illustrated by Jerry Pinkney and published by Dial.

From Van Dyke Parks and Malcolm Jones come *Jump!* (1986) *Jump Again!* (1987) and *Jump on Over!* (1989) all illustrated by Barry Moser and published by Harcourt Brace.

African-American Life Through History

Donald Crews, **Bigmama's**. Greenwillow, 1991. 32pp.

Simply written memories of Crews's childhood summers at his grandmother's house in the Florida countryside include the three-day train ride south, the outhouse, the pump for water, the farm animals, and most of all the fun and the warm family togetherness.

Double-page watercolor scenes emit the sort of joy only possible in the memories of middle age. Crews fills the pages with clearly rendered episodes that make explicit what the words only hint at, adding myriad details like the jumbled wood-pile, the shelves of accumulated tools and junk in the toolshed, the old wagon in the barn. Bold-faced text and all sorts of happy activities of the youngsters complete each scene. K-Grade 3.

___, **Shortcut**. Greenwillow, 1992. 32pp.

Same cast of youngsters as in *Bigmama's*, same setting, but this is a single adventure involving meeting a train at dusk while taking a risky shortcut. Crews's illustration of the approaching headlight beam containing its sound (Whoo) and then the passing ghost-like cars with Klakety-Klak-Klak written large below (and echoed on the end-papers) is especially imaginative and scary. K-Grade 3.

Deborah Hopkinson, **Sweet Clara and the Freedom Quilt**. Illustrated by James Ransome. Knopf, 1993. 36pp.

Set on a plantation in slavery days, the lengthy story of the quilt is told by Clara, the young slave seamstress who made it. Learning to sew helped her move from field work to the Big House, where she first heard of the Underground Railroad and the need for a map of it. She begins using scraps of cloth and the pieces of information she can collect to make a quilt showing the route to freedom. She leaves the quilt behind for others when she and Jack flee, first to find her mother, then on to freedom in Canada.

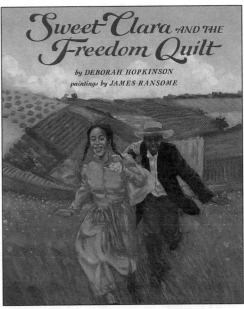

From *Sweet Clara and the Freedom Quilt* by Deborah Hopkinson. Illustrated by James Ransome. Copyright 1993. Reprinted with permission of Knopf.

The focus is on the people, in paintings that give personalities to characters while incorporating mere suggestions of interiors or impressions of landscape. Opaque paints are used like clay to model forms rather than to define them with detail. Episodes build visually as Clara works on her quilt, which is displayed on the endpapers. Ransome's visualizations add considerably to the narrative's exciting pace. Grades 2-5 or 6.

Elizabeth Fitzgerald Howard, **Aunt Flossie's Hats (and Crab Cakes Later)**. Illustrated by James Ransome. Clarion, 1991. 32pp.

This simply told family tale of Sarah and Susan's Sunday visits with great-great-aunt Flossie is inspired by the author's aunt and a real family experience. As described by Susan, the day includes play with the famous hats, lots of family love, and of course, crabcakes.

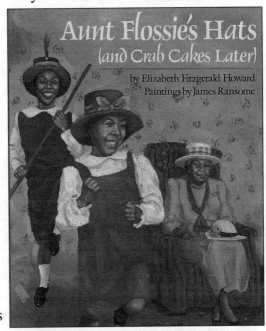

From *Aunt Flossie's Hats* by Elizabeth Fitzgerald Howard. Illustrated by James Ransome. Copyright 1991. Reprinted with permission of Clarion.

Ransome's oil paintings, mostly full-page but with a few vignettes on the text pages, describe a middle-class world filled with family affection. Details of interiors, a park, and a restaurant, with a couple of historical double-page scenes thrown in, are painted to emphasize character rather than realistic specificity. But the faces get special attention as they define each personality. K-Grade 3.

___, **Mac and Marie & the Train Toss Surprise**. Illustrated by Gail Gordon Carter. Four Winds, 1993.

Mac and Marie's excited anticipation of the passing of the train on which their Uncle Clem works in the diner, and from which he has promised to toss the surprise for them, is matched by the excitement of receiving and opening it. That their uncle cannot hope to ever be the engineer because of his race is stated; however, Mac can hope he will be one some day.

Carter's watercolor and colored pencil illustrations on double pages are mostly literal depictions of the events in the text, with some awkwardness in the figures. Compare with Ransome's to see what each adds to Howard's stories. Grades 1 or 2-4.

Dolores Johnson, **Now Let Me Fly: The Story of a Slave Family**. Macmillan, 1993. 32pp.

Johnson uses a narrator named Minna to tell the fictional story of a girl who is captured in Africa in 1815 and sold as a slave. Minna later marries Amadi, her companion on the slave ship, but after they have four children he is sold away, as is her son Joshua. When the master whips her daughter Sally, Minna sends her North to freedom. Her younger son goes to live with the Seminoles in Florida. Minna and her youngest daughter only dream of freedom. In an epilogue Johnson imagines possible futures for the family based on history. The text is lengthy, but simply and clearly written.

Conceived almost as a series of stills from a film, some in small rectangles, others full-page scenes, the illustrations include three particularly forceful double-page settings, like the shackled slaves on a long march, and the jubilant arrival in free Pennsylvania. Oil paints are used to block in forms and emphasize the emotional content of scenes such as the joyful "jump the broom" marriage or the mother's pleading to keep her son. The artist provides visual information to help us sense the slave experience. Grades 2-5.

Margaret King Mitchell, **Uncle Jed's Barbershop**. Illustrated by James Ransome. Simon & Schuster, 1993. 32pp.

Mitchell tells her story of life in the South in the 1920s and 30s in the voice of Sarah Jean, whose favorite Uncle Jed was the only black barber in the county. He travelled around to cut hair, since he had no shop, but he knew just what his shop would look like when he finally saved enough money to open it. When five-year-old Sarah Jean needs an operation, Uncle Jed gives $300 from his dream fund. A few years later, a Depression bank failure takes his savings and defers his dream again. At 79 he finally sees it come true, and dies happy. Mitchell simply and matter-of-factly discusses such unpleasant historic facts as segregated restrooms, water fountains, schools, and hospital services as part of her otherwise warm picture of the African-American life in that time and place.

Ransome's double-page oil paintings bring us into a rural world peopled with individuals who care about each other. He shows us the life of the period through items like a pot-bellied stove, a segregated doctor's office, an iron frame bed. Uncle Jed's portraits are especially insightful. The wallpaper pattern that appears on the endpapers is used as a unifying theme in several rooms of Sarah Jean's house and eventually also in Jed's barbershop. The patchwork quilt on her bed is a glorious creation; the animated Dalmatian is surely drawn from life. Grades 1 or 2-5.

Gloria Jean Pinkney, **Back Home**. Illustrated by Jerry Pinkney. Dial, 1992. 40pp.

The author has drawn on her own and family experiences for this long text describing Ernestine's trip from the city where she lives to the North Carolina farm where she was born. After her aunt and uncle welcome her she goes to sleep in her mother's old bedroom. Cousin Jack gives her a hard time at first, but relents. Ernestine joins in the life of the family, goes to church, and to put flowers on her grandmother's grave. When she leaves, she looks forward to returning the next summer to her family home.

The use of a cream-colored page rather than white helps give the artist's watercolors a nostalgic quality. As usual, Pinkney creates individuals who are full of human feeling and emotional content. Both the experiences and illustrations of this story are interesting to compare with those of Donald Crews, above. Grades 1-4.

Chris Raschka, **Charlie Parker Played Be Bop**. Orchard, 1992. 32pp.

There is no real story, just a few words per page, in this tone poem that plays with typeface and imagery to try to make the reader hear Parker's music. Charcoal and watercolors are blended to depict Parker playing his saxophone, while shoes strut by, along with lollipops and a black cat as spectator. The visuals here are a boldly funky narrative. K-Grade 3.

Faith Ringgold, **Aunt Harriet's Railroad in the Sky**. Crown, 1992. 32pp.

___, **Tar Beach**. Crown, 1991. (Caldecott Honor book) 32pp.

For *Tar Beach* Ringgold takes us back, in a deceptively brief, simple story, to her memories of the roof-tops of Harlem in the 1930s, where the tar on the roof became her beach on hot summer nights. There Cassie's imagination flies her above the city, the George Washington Bridge, the union building her father helps construct, even the ice cream factory. She'd like to change the discrimination her father faces because he's black, the tears her mother cries when he looks for work and "doesn't come home." Meanwhile she finds the freedom she seeks flying away "among the stars." A long addendum details the history on which her story is based. It also describes the quilt Ringgold created about *Tar Beach*, now in the Guggenheim Museum in New York, pictured in its entirety at the end of the story. Parts of the quilt's border run along the bottoms of the pages, tying the narrative together.

Some of the qualities of decorative patterning picked up from the border appear in the lights on the bridge, the windows of the ice cream factory, in the panoply of apartment houses, in Mommy's quilt, and in the dining room's braided rug. A few details of city life appear on the roof where the family gathers to eat picnic food amid the plants and drying laundry. The magic is in the scenes of Cassie's flying, arms akimbo, pigtails straight out. There's a child-like simplicity to the paintings in keeping with the directness of the text. But the compositions reveal the artist's sensibility. Grades 1-6.

Cassie and her brother Be Be fly again in *Aunt Harriet's Underground Railroad...*, this time to the days of slavery in the South. Cassie learns from Harriet Tubman something of the hardships of her ancestors, and of the Underground Railroad that helps them to freedom. Ringgold's illustrations are in a similar style to those in *Tar Beach*, but not connected by the quilt motif. They also reveal more history in their details. Grades 2-6.

Irene Smalls-Hector, **Irene and the Big, Fine Nickel**. Illustrated by Tyrone Geter. Little, Brown, 1991. 32pp.

The author draws upon her own experiences growing up in Harlem in the 1950s to detail the events of a sunny Saturday in the life of seven-year-old Irene. While her mother sleeps and her younger brothers and sisters are away, she gets herself up, goes out to play, argues with Charlene, plays in the park with her friends Lulamae and Lulabelle, plants some seeds, finds a glorious nickel to buy a raisin bun to share, makes up with Charlene, and still has a wonderful day to look forward to. With a lengthy text full of the details that make the time and place come alive, this shows us the Harlem where "nobody locked the door and you never questioned being black because there were a million people who looked just like you."

Full-page opaque paintings illustrate aspects of the facing text pages, actions that are the focus of the elaborate conversations. The settings show interiors and street scenes unmentioned in the words, in ways that provide a specificity of place, like the signs that cover store fronts, or the furniture in Irene's apartment home. Painted rather than drawn, the pictures create atmosphere broadly. In particular the children are depicted engaging in activities natural to spirited youngsters. K-Grade 3.

Sherley Anne Williams, **Working Cotton**. Illustrated by Carole Byard. Harcourt Brace, 1992. (Caldecott Honor book) 32pp.

In a spare text written in Black English and based on her poetry and her childhood experience, Williams tells of a day in the life of a migrant family who pick cotton. Shelan, too small to have her own sack but big enough to help, tells of the smells, the sights, the long hard day, the fatigue at the end.

Acrylic paintings totally fill the wide double pages with expressionistic pictures that provide the soul for Shelan's bare bones descriptions. We can feel the speed of her Daddy's picking in the diagonal of his sack and his leaning forward across both pages. The beauty of the cotton fields as visualized stands ironically in opposition to the sweat-dripping faces of the family and the dawn-to-dusk workday. We see the bus ride in the dark that starts the story and in the final scene of the workers leaving the fields with their bodies reflecting the redness of the setting sun. Close-ups focus attention on the human scale of the endless labor. K-Grade 3 or 4.

Jeanette Winter, **Follow the Drinking Gourd**. Knopf, 1988. 48pp.

Winter tells how the actual song taught by the sailor Peg Leg Joe helps fictional characters to follow the route of the Underground Railroad to freedom. When her husband James is about to be sold away from her, Molly remembers the song and sees the "gourd" or Dipper in the sky. She, James, and three others follow the trail as described in the verses of the song until they reach the Ohio River, where Peg Leg Joe takes them across and sends them on through other secret houses to Canada. The song is reproduced in the book. Added notes further describe the Underground Railroad, the white sailor Peg Leg Joe, and how the song worked to guide the runaways.

The formality of the layout tends, by contrast with the more vernacular text, to accentuate the emotional content of the visual narrative. Opaque paint is used in a flat manner to create a series of longish rectangular scenes, each framed with a thin black line and set on the white page. The text is most often placed below, but sometimes on a page facing the illustration. The family is shown involved with a series of adventures, frightening and friendly, but always together so we perceive them as a solid unit. There is a mythic quality in the visualization, as shapes are abstracted to create patterns in the clouds, rows of corn, ripples on a river. Even the Big Dipper constellation is depicted as a dipper. Grades 1 or 2-4.

Two heavily texted stories in picture book format about real people add to the African-American experience. Gwen Everett's *John Brown: One Man Against Slavery* (Rizzoli, 1993) has reproductions of Jacob Lawrence's series of heavily abstracted opaque gouache paintings using stencil-like forms and exaggerated gestures for dramatic illustrations of her story of Brown's raid on Harper's Ferry as told through the eyes of a young girl.

Alan Schroeder's *Ragtime Tumpie* (Little Brown, 1989) is a lively account of the childhood of Josephine Baker in turn-of-the-century St. Louis, dancing to the ragtime music she heard everywhere. Bernie Fuchs's textured paintings glow with yellows, oranges and browns, with one in the "blues," and are filled with real characters in motion in the place and time. A note fills in some information on Baker.

African Americans Today

There are so many picture books with African-American characters in print and being published that we cannot possibly deal with them all. We have tried to examine above those dealing with subjects particularly relevant to African-American culture. We would like to list some examples of picture books by fine illustrators, just one from each, that tell good stories with characters that happen to be African American, but could be simply American. By illustrator, they include:

Floyd Cooper:
Eloise Greenfield, **Grandpa's Face**. Putnam/Philomel, 1988.

Pat Cummings:
Clean Your Room, Harvey Moon! Bradbury, 1991.

Jan Spivey Gilchrist:
Eloise Greenfield, **William and the Good Old Days**. HarperCollins, 1993.

Jonathan Green:
Denize Lauture, **Father and Son**. Philomel, 1993.

Dolores Johnson:
Your Dad Was Just Like You. Macmillan, 1993.

Jerry Pinkney:
Valerie Flournoy, **The Patchwork Quilt**. Dial, 1985.

James Ransome:
Denise Lewis Patrick, **Red Dancing Shoes**. Tambourine, 1993.

David Soman:
Angela Johnson, **The Leaving Morning**. Orchard, 1992.
All 32pp.

Section 6
The Caribbean and Latin America

Large numbers of immigrants have come to the United States from Mexico, Central and South America, and the Caribbean. Indeed, Spanish is a second language in many American cities today. Even the Spanish varies enormously, however, because of the differences in the countries from which the speakers come. In some small areas, French, sometimes also Creole, is spoken as a souvenir of the French explorers and settlers. The Spanish and Portuguese invaders imposed their language and Hispanic culture upon many peoples who were living in the Caribbean and Latin America, making for a history of conflict and conquest that has left scars similar to those we have in North America. A rich variety of myths and legends also comes from this many-faceted mixture, as do distinctive arts and crafts. It is necessary, as with Africa, to use a map, and try to speak of a specific area and people when discussing these cultures with children.

Unfortunately there is little in picture books about life in these individual Latin American countries today, or about the experiences of these particular immigrants and their struggles.

The Caribbean

Original Tales and Folk Tales of the Past

Note: Stories of the Anansi character from Africa are told by African Americans throughout the Americas as well. Some picture books, however, have illustrations with no particular cultural characteristics, so they are not listed.

George Crespo, **How the Sea Began: A Taino Myth**. Clarion, 1993. 32pp.

"In the beginning of time" there was no sea, just land and four great mountains. On one, called Boriquen, lived Yaya and his wife Ita with their son, a skilled hunter called Yayael with a magic bow that enabled him always to bring back game. When he is caught in a hurricane, only his bow and arrows are found to be placed in the burial gourd hung in the hut. When he looks inside, Yaya finds fish. Curious boys break the gourd, from which salty water and fish flow until Boriquen is an island. Now the people need not go hungry, for they can always have fish. The author discusses the background of the creation tale in his note, explaining the beginning of Puerto Rico, and some customs of the Taino.

Scenes of the life style of hunters and of basic agriculture are given a dramatic rendering with textured oil paintings. Full page settings and vignettes combine naturalistic objects with more fanciful and visually inventive scenes, such as the sculptured clouds of the hurricane and Yayael's name appearing in the sky as his mother cries out. Grades 1 or 2-4.

Fiona French, **Anancy and Mr. Dry-Bone**. Little, Brown, 1991. 28pp.

French has used the traditional title characters from Caribbean and African folklore for her simply told original story in a Caribbean setting. Rich Mr. Dry-Bone and poor Anancy both want to marry clever and beautiful Miss Louise. She has never laughed, so will wed whoever can make her laugh. Mr. Dry-Bone tries all his tricks in vain. When Anancy borrows from the animals, his absurd get-up brings laughter and Miss Louise as his bride.

The intricate black borders with ornate silhouettes frame windows and set the tone for double pages of inventive visual fireworks. Black dominates in all sorts of patterns, especially geometric shapes. There are colored stripes on Anancy's otherwise black outfit, with matching stripes on his socks. Miss Louise's black peasant-type dress is complemented by a red and yellow kerchief. There's a brilliantly feathered parrot on the branch of a black-leafed tree, and so on. Design is queen here, each page bringing a new set of patterns. Costumes and architecture suggest a carefree place where natives love to dance. Grades 2-4.

Richardo Keens-Douglas, **The Nutmeg Princess**. Illustrated by Annouchka Galouchko. Annick Press (paper), 1992. 32pp.

Although told in many words and small print, this legend-like tale of Grenada, "the Isle of Spice" and the author's childhood home, is a simple one. A boy named Aglo and his friend Petal decide to try to see the beautiful Nutmeg Princess in the volcanic lake high up the mountain. Only old Petite Mama, a hard-working farmer feared by the townspeople, has ever seen the Princess. Aglo sees her also, but no one believes him. Still, since she is supposed to have diamonds, the people go to the lake out of greed. Only to Aglo, and then to Petal, does the Princess reveal herself. Because she cares for her friend, Petal receives a diamond and the blessing of the Princess. Then Petite Mama disappears, leaving her farm and precious nutmeg trees to the good care of Aglo and Petal.

The pictures seem to be made as if with tiny stitches in a soft textile. But they are gouache-painted visual fantasies in which the characters of the story coexist with all sorts of trees and animals. All colors are intense, and seem even more so because they are juxtaposed with so many others. Like some styles of folk art which these pictures resemble, there are no laws of perspective followed; some things are rendered naturalistically while most are treated like mystic icons. The illustrations fit with the fanciful story. Grades 1 or 2-4.

The Caribbean Today

Nancy White Carlstrom, **Baby-O**. Illustrated by Sucie Stevenson. Little, Brown, 1992. 32pp.

Rhythmic sounds punctuate a song-like verse describing family life and activities on a Caribbean island, as the farmer, the basketmaker, and the fisherman all load items on the jitney on its way to market.

An oceanside landscape with palm trees sets the scene; a decorated bus filled with casually clad passengers all heading for the open-air market completes the picture. Black lines define all shapes, while thin watercolors leave lots of space as they combine to create loose, light-hearted scenes that are meant to make us smile. K-Grades 2 or 3.

Lulu Delacre, **Vejigante/Masquerader**. Scholastic, 1993. 40pp.

The author has drawn from her childhood memories of Carnival in Puerto Rico to write the story, in English and Spanish, of young Ramon. He has worked and saved to buy the materials necessary to make his costume to be a masquerader, who can play tricks for all of February with never a reprimand. With extra work he will also be able to afford a special mask from the maskmaker. Finally Ramon is ready to march with the other masqueraders, especially El Gallo's group. But an old goat shreds his costume, ruining his chances for the rest of Carnival time. Luckily his mother can help him mend it so he can continue the fun and excitement of being a *vejigante*.

Exploiting mixed media in a variety of page formats, Delacre depicts Ramon's environment with attention to such details as the naked suspended light bulb in his room and the row of clapboard houses on his street. Most attention is given to the costumes and horned masks of the *vejigantes*, with swirling cloaks and swinging cow bladders. The illustrations express the preparations and the excitement of the celebration. The final pages of the book include more information on this and other similar festivals, chants, a glossary, and instructions for making a mask. K or Grades 1-4.

Lynn Joseph, **An Island Christmas**. Illustrated by Catherine Stock. Clarion, 1992. 32pp.

This author has drawn upon her own and her mother's recollections of Christmas in Trinidad for this story of a young girl and her middle-class family preparing for the holiday. Told in dialect—"De sky blue for so"—and partially in verse, the tale includes gathering sorrel fruit for a special drink, making

From *Baby-O* by Nancy White Carlstrom. Illustrated by Sucie Stevenson. Copyright 1992. Reprinted with permission of Little, Brown.

From *Vejigante/Masqerader* by Lulu Delacre. Copyright 1993. Reprinted with permission of Scholastic.

The Caribbean and Latin America

black currant cake, and enjoying the music of the traditional *parang* band. There are added notes on the place, food, and customs.

Considerable attention is given to details in Stock's watercolors: the family's clothes, the corrugated tin roofs on the village shops, the flower-patterned tablecloth, the nailheads in the broad steps to a tree house. The double-page pictures bring a touch of tropical joy with their airiness and loving interaction of people. Grades 1-4.

___, **Coconut Kind of Day: Island Poems**. Illustrated by Sandra Speidel. Lothrop, 1990. 32pp.

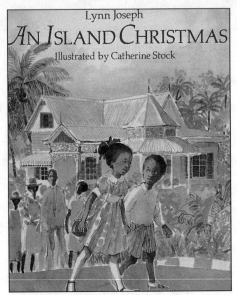

From *An Island Christmas* by Lynn Joseph. Illustrated by Catherine Stock. Copyright 1992. Reprinted with permission of Clarion.

Although each poem on a double-page spread is separate, together they give a picture of the daily activities, sights, sounds, and tastes of the life the author recalls from her Trinidad childhood. She goes to school, her mother to market, the fishermen fish, the steel band plays, and the *jumbi* man threatens as night falls. Young children will enjoy the language and understand the activities, while the older can appreciate the poetry. Joseph's added notes explain certain words and give more about her life as a child.

Wide double pages offer plenty of room for the short poems and evocative pictures. Each is a scene of an aspect of island life, from a cricket game to an ice cream vendor. Using pastels on a rough board produces an overall graininess that tends to suggest rather than make explicit the people and objects. This technique reinforces the mood, the quality of the good life by the sea. We see the lush vegetation and the friendly folk as perceived by young girls in blue and white school uniforms. K-Grade 5.

Joseph has also written *A Wave in Her Pocket: Stories from Trinidad* (Clarion, 1991), a 51-page collection for older students (grades 3-6) with Brian Pinkney's scratchboard illustrations.

Frane Lessac, **My Little Island**. Lippincott, 1984, Harper Trophy paper, 1987. 40pp.
As a young boy describes his visit with a friend to the Caribbean island of Monserrat where he was born, he includes the food, animals, markets, landscape, even his school, carnival time, and the volcano that sometimes smokes.

Presented as a picture album, each page of text faces a picture that deals with its subject. In fact, each original painting was done for exhibit; many are listed as in collections. We see the "boats filled with flipping and flopping fish," the shelves of canned goods in the shop. Endpapers show the island as a child might see it, painted without perspective, mountains covered with palm trees, whales spouting off shore. The style is naive, the poses stiff, but there are details of local life and good-natured feeling galore. K-Grade 2 or 3.

Lessac has also written and illustrated *Caribbean Canvas* (Lippincott, 1987) where her poems in island dialect are illustrated with reproductions of her paintings of the island in a similar style but with fewer details. Still useful for additional background.

Rita Phillips Mitchell, **Hue Boy**. Illustrated by Caroline Binch. Dial, 1993. 28pp.

The author, who grew up in Belize, has based this story about a boy on a Caribbean island on the experience of a nephew in Belize. The text has a repetitious refrain that children enjoy. Hue Boy doesn't seem to grow "at all, at all." His schoolmates tease; he feels bad. His mama tries feeding him extra food, his gran gives him larger clothes to grow into, he tries to stretch himself, even visits the wise man and healing woman of the village. But nothing helps until his father, who has been working on a ship, comes home. Then he's so happy he doesn't "feel small at all, at all" any more.

The cover is an appealing portrait of our hero, all smiles and gleaming eyes. The endpapers present his lush, tropical environment. Watercolor paints that exploit the white of the paper to produce a sun-drenched world are also manipulated to create humans with genuine character. The illustrations form a page of sequenced vignettes showing Hue Boy's exercises to a double-page scene of him in school with his uniformed classmates. There is just enough detail to evoke the sense of place and the pace of life we associate with the Caribbean. K-Grade 3.

Carmen Santiago Nodar, **Abuelita's Paradise**. Illustrated by Diane Paterson. Whitman, 1992. 32pp. Also published in Spanish.

In her grandmother's rocking chair Marita remembers the stories she was told about grandmother's childhood in Puerto Rico, where her father worked in the sugar cane fields and they lived out on a farm. To her grandmother, it was "paradise," to which Marita hopes she has returned now that she has died. Her memory and love live on, as Marita hopes to visit Puerto Rico some day and see it all.

From *Abuelita's Paradise* by Carmen Santiago Nodar. Illustrated by Diane Paterson. Copyright 1992. Reprinted with permission of Whitman.

The transparent watercolors create scenes appropriate for these sentimental childhood memories and dreams. They are detailed enough to show the cane fields and ox carts, sunset seen from the porch, riding on a mule through the lush countryside, and even flying in grandmother's rocker along with a couple of flamingos. Varied picture size with lots of white space for the text. Grades 1-4.

Katherine Orr, **My Grandpa and the Sea**. Carolrhoda, 1990. 32pp.

Lila remembers her grandfather, a fisherman on the island of St. Lucia, in his dugout canoe. When fish become scarce, he tries to do other things, but misses his life where he feels God lives, on the sea. He finally begins to cultivate scarce sea moss in special frames, and can thus return to the life he loves. Lila has gone away to school but never forgotten him and the lessons he taught. A simply told, sentimental story.

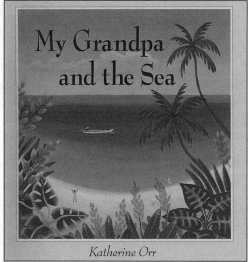

From *My Grandpa and the Sea* by Katherine Orr. Copyright 1990. Reprinted with permission of Carolrhoda.

Smoothly appled opaque paints create full-page pictures and attractive vignettes on facing text pages. Details of everyday life and backgrounds of local seascape and landscape specify time and place. People are portrayed in a simplified but appealing fashion, especially Grandpa. K or Grades 1-4.

Charlotte Pomerantz, **The Chalk Doll**. Illustrated by Frane Lessac. Lippincott, 1989.

When Rose must stay in bed with a cold, her mother tells her about life in Jamaica when the mother was a child: rag dolls, milk, presents, shoes she had to do without. Although she has "chalk dolls," which are white dolls from a store, Rosa asks to make a rag doll like the one her mother had.

Lessac's style, as described above in *My Little Island*, illuminates the many details of life in the mother's childhood in a small town. K-Grade 4.

Latin America

Original Tales and Folk Tales of the Past

Manlio Argueta, **Magic Dogs of the Volcanoes/Los Perros Magicos de los Volanes**. Translated by Stacey Ross. Illustrated by Elly Simmons. Children's Book Press, 1990. 32pp.

This bilingual original story based on the traditional "magic dogs" of El Salvador was written for the children of El Salvador by a noted native author. After describing how the people love the *cadejos*, or magic dogs, that always protect them, the tale relates how a wicked man and his brothers try to destroy the *cadejos* who stop the men from exploiting their workers. The lead soldiers they send almost succeed, until the volcanoes come to the rescue of the *cadejos*.

Full-page paintings are crammed with heavy black-outlined figures and abstract representations of trees, landscape, and the two key mountains. They and the sun have human faces. The lead soldiers look the part in fancy red and blue uniforms. The pages intermix people, objects, and text in ways that emphasize the emotional content of the symbols rather than their more literal spacial relations. This form of surrealism is appropriate to the political situation in El Salvador, which probably underlies this story. K-Grades 3 or 4.

John Bierhorst, translator, **Spirit Child: A Story of the Nativity**. Illustrated by Barbara Cooney. Mulberry (paper), 1990. 32pp.

This 400-year-old retelling of the Nativity story with Aztec cultural influences has been rediscovered in Aztec and now translated. The text is extensive, making this a marginal picture book, although the language is not too complex. The story is familiar, with some local additions and many reverent passages.

The landscapes, artifacts, costumes, and vegetation are suggestive of the time and place of the story. The full-page scene of the Dead Land ruled by skeletons has the special flavor of some Mexican folk art. Cooney's use of smoothly applied opaque paints softens her figures so that they take on Western qualities despite their Aztec looks, black hair, and brown skins. The scene of joyous flying angels could come from a Renaissance ceiling. Yet the tale is indeed the combination of a priest's notion of the Bible and local lore. One might think of the pictures as translations just as the text is translated. Grades 2 or 3-6.

Donald Charles, **Chancay and the Secret of Fire: A Peruvian Folktale**. Putnam, 1992. 32pp.

From his study of ancient Peruvian art and culture, Charles has written an original tale of pre-Inca times with a hero named Chancay, like the name of one ancient Peruvian culture. The story is one that appears in many cultures—a hero brings his people the gift of fire. With the aid of Tambo, Spirit of Father Earth, whom he has caught and released, Chancay goes through trials to prove that he is brave and strong as well as kind. Then he is able to steal the moon's golden mirror and catch the fire of the sun.

Endpapers reproduce some of the symbols used in the story, in a style that is influenced by pre-Incan Peruvian designs. The title pages introduce the colors of the mixed media used as well as the stylized approach to landscape and figure: all is smoothed out, flat, and decorated. There is a hint of the use of geometric shapes seen in the work of Gerald McDermott, and of the encapsulated forms seen in native cultures of the U.S. Northwest Coast. K or Grades 1-4.

Stefan Czernecki and Timothy Rhodes, **Pancho's Pinata**. Illustrated by Stefan Czernecki. Hyperion, 1992. 40pp.

This simply told Christmas story of Mexico was inspired by the Diego Rivera mural "La Piñata and Procession" of 1953, and by time spent in Mexico. During the *posada*, the traditional Mexican Christmas procession to re-enact Joseph and Mary's quest for lodging, in the center of San Miguel, a tiny star coming to watch gets stuck on a large cactus. When a small boy sets it free, its twinkle brings him happiness through the years. As an old man wanting to bring this joy to others, he makes the first *piñata*, or jar full of gifts, for the children. The background information about the *piñata* is in an afterword.

Gouache paintings here look like posters as their flat shapes are carefully composed inside ornate borders. Mission-style architecture, sandals and sombreros, yucca and cactus, straw toys and the star-shaped *piñata* all bring a sanitized Mexico to mind. The colors are pure, the tile roofs perfectly even and unbroken. The simplicity of religious faith in the text is matched in the neatness of the pictures. K or Grades 1-4.

Stefan Czernecki and Timothy Rhodes, **The Sleeping Bread**. Illustrated by Stefan Czernecki. Hyperion, 1992. 40pp.

Longer than the usual picture book, this tale of a baker in a small Guatemalan village, where his shop was the scene of a "miracle," was spun by the authors from their experiences with the life and art of the country. Beto always gave bread and company to the beggar Zafiro. The townspeople did not want a beggar around to spoil their festival, so they ask him to leave. A tear falls into Beto's baking jar as Zafiro says goodbye. For days after, the bread will not rise. At the shrine of San Simeon, Beto's dream tells him he must bring Zafiro back. The return does wake the "sleeping bread," to the joy of all.

Gouache is used here to make full-page bordered paintings similar to those in *Pancho's Piñata*. But where the Mexican citizens wore white, these Guatemalans wear ornate patterns, which are picked up in representations of fields and in furniture and pottery. The final festival scene is like a visual orchestra with all instruments at full blast. K or Grades 1-4.

James de Sauza, **Brother Anansi and the Cattle Ranch/El Hermano Anansi y el Rancho de Ganado**. Adapted by Harriet Rohmer. Spanish version by Rosalma Zubizarreta. Illustrated by Stephen von Mason. Children's Book Press, 1989. 32pp.

The stories of Anansi, the folk hero/trickster we have met before, are told by African Americans throughout the Americas. Here, from the coast of Nicaragua, Anansi learns that Tiger has won the lottery. He invites Tiger to buy cattle and set up a ranch with him. When business is going well, Anansi decides it's time to divide the animals. He tricks Tiger out of almost all of them. Notes give background information on both the story and the illustrations.

Highly stylized pictures have figures, trees, objects all painted in flat, intense colors with black outlines. Gestures are stiff and exaggerated; everything seems humorously out of proportion. In contrast, the cattle are rendered naturalistically. There is an overall slapstick comic effect. Grades 1-4.

Lois Ehlert, **Moon Rope/Un Lazo a la Luna**. Harcourt, Brace, 1992. 32pp.

In this legend told in two languages, Fox and Mole try to reach the moon. They can't make their woven grass rope reach, until the birds help. But Mole slips, falls back to earth, and is so upset he prefers to stay in his hole underground thereafter. Whether Fox makes it remains a question. Notes detail the source of the story and the inspiration for the illustrations.

Motifs influenced by Peruvian crafts have been modified into sharply defined symbols made of cut-out shapes with lots of silver and red. These are set against solid, intensely colored backgrounds to illustrate aspects of the brief text. Large-size pages with stunning pictures reflect some of the mysticism of the ancient Peruvian art objects. K-Grade 4.

Flora, **Feathers Like a Rainbow: An Amazon Indian Tale**. Harper, 1989. 25pp.

Flora's Brazilian great-grandfather's writings on the Amazon Indians were the source of this simply told *porquoi* legend, explaining how the birds of the Amazon rain forest got their colorful feathers. A gray-winged trumpeter bird tries to satisfy her son Jacamin's desire for color like that of the flowers around them. When other birds find hummingbird's secret of colors, they take them for themselves, leaving nothing for Jacamin but the purple he has on his breast today.

From her naturalist great-grandfather and from the director of the Royal Botanic Gardens at Kew, Flora has gathered the information necessary to illustrate the flora and fauna of the rain forest. Double pages are filled with tree trunks or masses of blossoms and birds of every sort. The colors are applied thickly, in a fuzzy manner, often suggesting pastels. The textures of feathers, flower petals, berries, all tend to resemble each other in an overall bushiness. The appeal is visceral; one can almost feel the jungle's congestion and fecund fullness. Budding botanists should enjoy checking the accuracy of the many plants and birds presented. K-Grade 4.

Matthew Gollub, **The Twenty-five Mixtec Cats**. Illustrated by Leovigildo Martinez. Tambourine, 1993. 32pp.

In this original story "based on the folklore of Oaxaca," a healer is given 25 kittens in a Mixtec market. Since he takes no money for his healing, and his village has no cats, he hopes to sell them. But nobody wants to feed them. The neighbors, fearing the cats will cause trouble, ask the evil healer of the village to get rid of them. When she fails and they complain, she curses the butcher, who becomes ill. The good healer saves the butcher by taking the curse of the evil healer upon himself. He is saved by the cats, whom the villagers then finally accept. Notes add information about Oaxaca and about the artist.

A distinctive sense of design shapes the watercolor-painted pages in tans, yellows, and pinks. What appear as borders are in good measure pictures that help tell the story, although sometimes they contain isolated images relating to the environment in general: houses, animals, trees. Scenes are housed in rectangles as if they were superimposed. The straightforward text appears in other rectangles, sometimes washed with color. Figures are fully modeled, with wrinkles and shadows helping to create solid bodies and animated faces that are more caricatured than realistic. The costume and background do reflect the Oaxaca area. Grades 1-4.

Deborah Nourse Lattimore, **The Flame of Peace: A Tale of the Aztecs**. Harper, 1987, Trophy (paper), 1991. 40pp.

Since little is known of Aztec mythology beyond the names of their gods, Lattimore has "tried to combine the known elements and the lively, authentic art with some educated guesses based on my research and knowledge of the period" in a story of a young boy outwitting the traditional nine evil lords of darkness to bring a New Fire of peace from the Morning Star. As his city prepares for war, Two Flint sets out bravely through many trials to end the threatening strife with the torch he carries back to the temple.

Parchment-like paper, red frames, and conventionalized symbols show the influence of ancient Aztec codices and other graphic artifacts. Endpapers provide a visual dictionary of the symbols used in the illustrations, while the bars and circles of Aztec numbers accompany the usual page numbers to add even more flavor. Watercolors and black outlines recreate the ornate patterns of clothing, headdresses, buildings, indeed of all things natural or artificial. The frenetic layouts emphasize the strong emotive content of the spirited narrative. As in her *Why There Is No Arguing in Heaven*, below, Lattimore has done her homework in order to deliver a strong sense of Aztec authenticity. Grades 2-6.

___, Why There Is No Arguing in Heaven: A Mayan Myth. Harper, 1989. 32pp.

Lattimore has here combined several translations of the original Spanish version of the Mayan history of the creation. To stop the arguing of the other gods, Hunab Ku, the creator god, declares that whoever can create a being worthy of worshipping the gods would sit at his side. Attempts a making such men of mud and of wood fail. The spirits made by the Maize God succeed, so he sits by Hunab Ku. The author/illustrator describes the history of the material she worked from and her aim to impart the spirit of the Maya.

Paintings reproduce some of the symbolic character of the Mayan stone reliefs in tones of bluish gray to embellish the text pages. Facing, full-color pictures reminiscent of Mayan paintings use a few of the symbols as actors in scenes in Western style describing the events of the story. Endpapers are devoted to a visual dictionary produced in stony tones of blue, which is interesting to compare with the Aztec symbols in the author's *Flame of Peace* discussed above. Readers can note where the pictographs are used, as in page numbers. Strong emotional content here is based on imaginative interpretation of the original art forms. Grades 2-6.

Amanda Loverseed, **The Thunder King: A Peruvian Folk Tale**. (Folk Tales of the World) Bedrick/Blackie, 1991. 32pp.

This story is "inspired by the landscape and textiles of Peru," but has no base in Peruvian lore. Twin brothers usually work together, but one day Tantay stays to guard the crops from birds while Illanti goes up into the hills to watch the llamas. Impressed by his zeal, Thunder snatches Tantay, taking him to his palace to work for him. Illanti, with the help of Condor and the music of his pipes, rescues his brother.

Loverseed combines naturalistic watercolor scenes of the Peruvian highlands with more fanciful pictures of Thunder's activities. Each double-page illustration is bordered by a different band of pattern derived from local pottery or textiles. The endpapers also show stylized animals and bands of color. Local costumes, houses and llamas add cultural specificity.

Unfortunately Loverseed's paintings are uneven; although the scenes with Thunder amply express his potency and magic, her rendering of people is particularly problematic and awkward. Grades 1-4.

Harriet Rohmer, Octavio Chow, Morris Vidaure, **The Invisible Hunters/Los Cazadores Invisibles: A Legend from the Miskito Indians of Nicaragua**. Illustrated by Z. Children's Book Press, 1987, 32pp.

This tale in two languages incorporates the legendary creature called the Dar, traditional stories about invisible hunters, and the actual impact of the arrival of Europeans in the 17th century, as remembered by the Miskitos of Nicaragua. Three brothers are given invisibility by the Dar, so that they can hunt the warrior wild pig easily with sticks. They must promise never to sell the meat, only give it away, and never to hunt with guns. All goes well, the men and the village prosper, until traders come to buy meat despite the promise. Soon there's no longer enough left for the village, so the brothers are persuaded to use guns. They demand money from the villagers, who become angry. The hunters have so forgotten their promise that one day they are permanently invisible, and are banished. Some say they still wander, calling the Dar to make them visible again. Rohmer's extensive notes add more information on the source of the story and on contemporary problems in Nicaragua.

Using the simplest of cut paper shapes on the simplest of fingerpainted backgrounds, the artist expresses both the primal forces of the Miskito life style and the magic of the Dar. Marbleized papers, construction papers, and artist-prepared papers are cut with economy of detail and laid out for dramatic effect rather than specific cultural reference. Grades 1 or 2-5.

Susan Hand Shetterly, **The Dwarf-Wizard of Uxmal**. Illustrated by Robert Shetterly. Atheneum, 1990. 32pp.

Although no specific source is given, the publishers say this is a Maya legend from the Yucatan peninsula. The lengthy text is divided into chapters. Tol, the dwarf-wizard hatched from an egg and cared for by an old woman and a snake, has supernatural help when he challenges the governor of the city of Uxmal to contests. When terrible drought threatens everyone, and the governor's efforts fail to break it, Tol and his friends bring the rain. Finally, the governor challenges Tol to build a temple in one day. Only that will prove that Tol is the wizard that prophesy has declared will rule. The old woman's magic makes the building possible and thereafter a long reign.

Watercolor-painted scenes, including Mayan temples, warriors in costume and headdress derived from ancient carvings and paintings, and a few local buildings, help place the action in a jungle community like Uxmal. The illustrations come in various sizes. They tend to play up the comic aspects of Tol's adventures utilizing a Western approach to picture-making. There are a lot of close-ups; one of the governor's profile splendidly arrayed in plumed headdress and ornate neckpiece looks classically Mayan. Shetterly's interpretation of the Mayan style is interesting to compare with Lattimore's in *Why There Is No Arguing in Heaven* (Harper, 1989) above. Grades 2 or 3-6.

Beatriz Vidal, **The Legend of El Dorado: A Latin American Tale**. Adapted by Nancy Van Laan. Illustrated by Beatriz Vidal. Knopf, 1991. 34pp.

From the many legends of El Dorado or the gilded man, told to the arriving Spanish by the Native Americans of South America, Vidal has created a simple but many-faceted version to appeal to children. From the shores of Lake Guatavita the serpent of the lake has taken the queen of the Chibchas and her young daughter. The king is in despair. The priests consult the gods, then advise the king to rule wisely until it is his time to join his wife and child. To remind

From *The Legend of El Dorado* by Beatriz Vidal. Copyright 1991. Reprinted with permission of Knopf.

and honor the serpent, each year the king is covered with gold dust and cast with gold and jewels into the lake, until his time comes. Then he sinks into the lake without rising. The ritual is repeated by each new king, making the lake truly "dorado." Vidal's extensive introductory notes give more background information.

Vidal's decorative approach to visualizing the mythic jungle is exemplified in the endpapers festooned with florid birds entwined in leafy arabesques. The large double-page pictures exploit the ability of color pencils to create smoothly modeled forms in a manner that shows the spiritual unity of the people and the natural environment. Details of dress and buildings are generic to Latin America rather than culture-specific. The overall impression is one of a peaceful jungle kingdom that is appropriate for the tale. Grades 2-5.

Jane Anne Volkmer, **Song of the Chirimia: A Guatemalan Folktale/La Musica de la Chirimia: Folklore Guatemalteco**. Carolrhoda, 1990. 40pp.

In this bilingual retelling of a traditional story of a Mayan princess, Clear Sky is unmoved by a series of suitors for her hand until Black Feather, a simple young man, makes her smile with the beauty of his song. She sends him on a quest: before she will marry him he must match the beauty of the song of birds. With the help of Great Spirit, Black Feather makes a musical pipe called the *chirimia* to win the princess.

From *Song of the Chirimia* by Jane Anne Volkmer. Copyright 1990. Reprinted with permission of Carolrhoda.

The figures in the illustrations derive their forms and classical ornamentations from Mayan sources, mainly shown in profile to accentuate facial features and the elaborate headdresses. Conventional temples, palm trees, boats, and even the sounds coming from a player's pipes, reinforce the sense of history in the smoothly painted figures set against the white of the thickly texted pages. K or Grades 1-4.

David Wisniewski, **Rain Player**. Clarion, 1991. 32pp.

This original story is based on the art, language, traditions, and culture of the ancient Maya. In a time of drought, rash young Pik challenges the rain god Chac to a game of traditional ball. If Pik wins, the rains will come; if he loses, he will become a frog. With the help of the jaguar, the quetzal bird, and the ritual *cenote* or well, Pik succeeds. Many details of Mayan history and life are included in the authors's note.

Wisniewski's intricately cut paper illustrations, typical of his picture-making, create double-page scenes of dramatic intensity. Costumes with elaborate headdresses, jungles with animals, birds, and foliage, temples, all are incorporated into settings of great complexity. Grades 2 or 3-6.

Contemporary Latin American Life

Omar S. Castaneda, **Abuela's Weave**. Illustrated by Enrique O. Sanchez. Lee & Low, 1993. 32pp.

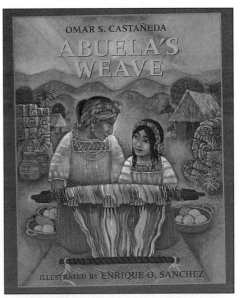

Writing about Guatemala, the country of his birth, the author tells how young Esperanza is learning from her *abuela* or grandmother, how to weave on the backstrap loom. They work hard together in the family compound to prepare for selling at the market during the Fiesta in Guate. Because she fears that her birthmarked face may deter customers, Abuela dresses unobtrusively in black and stays away from Esperanza. So the young girl must negotiate the bus ride, the busy city streets, putting her weavings on display, and the anxious wait for customers all by herself. Her intricate traditional weaving sells well, however, and the two return happily home together.

From *Abuela's Weave* by Omar S. Castaneda. Illustrated by Enrique O. Sanchez. Copyright 1993. Reprinted with permission of Lee & Low.

Acrylic paintings exploit their opaque intensities to produce scenes that depict the countryside and city with specificity: the river valley with thatched-roof houses, the bus, the city streets. But our focus, and Esperanza's, is on Abuela, with her hours of weaving under a magical tree, the fabric patterns of her blouse and headband. Text pages include fabric-design borders, while the splendor of the large tapestry also adds significance to this art form. The theme of love of grandmother and grandchild runs throughout, illuminated by gestures and glances. Grades 1-4.

Ted Lewin, **Amazon Boy**. Macmillan, 1993. 32pp.

In his original story about a young boy's first trip from his Amazon jungle home to the port city of Belem, the author includes facts about life on the river today with a plea for conservation to save what's left. Paulo and his father take the steamer downriver, admire the bounty of fish available although in diminishing size and numbers, and wander through the shops of the city. Paulo thinks deeply about what he has seen and what his father has told him about the disappearing jungle. When fishing after his return home, he lets loose a fish he has caught, as his small part to help save part of the bounty of the Amazon.

These watercolors of life on the Amazon River visualize the lushness of the vegetation, the boats that ply the river, Paulo's house up on a platform. The scenes of the fishing docks with their superabundance of fish, the fishermen, the customers, all are replete with the sounds and smells of the area. But the adjoining stalls of merchandise and black vultures are symbols of a grim future. Lewin's highly detailed pictures fill the double pages with real people in a specific place. His feelings about them are evident. K or Grades 1-4.

Harriet Rohmer, **Uncle Nacho's Hat/ El Sombrero del Tio Nacho**. Spanish by Rosalma Zubizarreta. Illustrated by Veg Reisberg. Children's Book Press, 1989. 32pp.

This story is a folk tale performed by the Puppet Workshop of Nicaraguan National Television. When his niece Ambrosia gives him a new hat, Uncle Nacho can't seem to get rid of his old one. People keep recognizing it and bringing it back. Finally he begins to follow Ambrosia's advice, thinks in new ways, and introduces his new hat to everyone.

Full-page illustrations face the bilingual text. Each picture is set in a unique border that includes objects associated with the scene. Opaque paints are used in a flat manner that frequently gives the impression of silk-screened shapes with sharp edges. The colors used are those associated with the tropics. Details include the vegetation and casual dress of the area. Humans and objects are stylized, simplified to include only their most fundamental shapes: cattle look like cookie-cut-outs. Perspective is exploited mostly for its enhancement of the design of the picture. There is a sense of light-hearted humor that parallels a narrative bordering on simplistic. K-Grade 4.

For more information on the culture of Mexican Americans, June Behrens's *Fiesta!: Cinco de Mayo* (Children's Press, 1986) offers a bit of history about the celebration of this holiday. Color photographs are by Scott Taylor.

Elizabeth Silverthorne's *Fiesta!: Mexico's Great Celebrations* (Millbrook, 1992) covers religious, patriotic, and other festivals celebrated by the three cultural groups: Indians, Spanish, and Mexicans. Quite a bit of information, along with drawings, map, glossary, and recipes.

The Immigrant Experience

Gloria Anzaldua, **Friends From the Other Side/Amigos del Otro Lado**. Illustrated by Consuelo Mendez. Children's Book Press, 1993. 32pp.

Both author and illustrator grew up near the Mexican border location of this story. Young Prietita sympathizes with and defends Joaquin, a "wetback" or illegal immigrant from Mexico, when other children taunt him. She helps him hide from the border patrol who would send him and his mother back to Mexico. The herb woman teaches Prietita how to find herbs and fix them to heal Joaquin's sores. The simple bilingual tale is full of the poverty and desperation of life on the U.S.-Mexican border, and of the kindnesses shown to others in need by those who have little themselves. Strong stuff for its reading level-age.

Mendez's paintings are realistic full-page depictions of people and setting, showing some not very pretty details of daily life along with portraits of the characters. Grades 2 or 3-6.

Denys Cazet, **Born in the Gravy**. Orchard, 1993. 32pp.

Although Cazet shows some of the wit of his *Never Spit on your Shoes* (Orchard, 1990), this is basically a serious story of the prejudice an immigrant girl faces from other children. From her father she gains the strength to come through. Cazet uses pastels to depict real people characters here instead of animals. Very moving and effective. Grades 1-4 or 5.

Bud Howlett's *I'm New Here* (Houghton Mifflin, 1993) is a report on Jazmin Escalante's first days in California after coming from El Salvador with her family. She speaks no English and is worried, but manages to come through. Color photographs make her experience real for children in grades 2-5.

<u>Notes</u>

Section 7
Aboriginal or "Native" Cultures of North America

As in Latin America and the Caribbean, exploring Europeans encountered a large number of groups already living in North America, each with its own culture, customs, and language. All seemed to share a respect for the natural world of which they felt themselves an integral part, rather than the idea of nature as an alien force to be placed under control. We have all heard how settlers thought they cleared or bought and "owned" land, a concept foreign to the native population. The treatment of this population by the Europeans has come to be seen as cruel and unjust; the history of the "discovery" and colonization period has been revised most recently during the controversial 500th anniversary celebration of the arrival of Christopher Columbus.

It is particularly difficult to rule on the authenticity of works about these groups. We have no accounts written by them from before the Conquest. We have many fewer surviving artifacts like the buildings and carvings from pre-Columbian Mexico and Central America. The forced resettlement and subsequent hardships have greatly reduced the populations and muddied the lines between one native group and another. Only a few groups now still speak the language of their ancestors. Meanwhile, similar artifacts and way of life may have falsely led us to group some, like Native Americans from the Plains or from the Northwest Coast, together. Recent attempts to revitalize tribal unity, ethnic pride, and the oral tradition can be seen in news reports as well as in the increasing number of picture books with Native American themes. The rising concern for the environment has also reinforced the original native sensitivity to nature. The struggle for recognition and power goes on; we can only try to help all children understand a little better this important cultural contribution to all our lives. On this continent, as in Africa and Latin America, there are a multitude of groups who have lived in different areas at different times in history, sometimes culturally or linguistically related and sometimes not. Children need to be shown this as carefully and accurately as possible from the research and facts now available.

Original Tales and Folk Tales of the Past

Shonto Begay, **Ma'ii and Cousin Toad: A Traditional Navajo Story**. Scholastic, 1992. 32pp.

When lazy coyote, the traditional trickster, tricks and swallows his hard-working "cousin," the horned toad, in order to take over toad's farm, toad makes him so miserable from inside that coyote leaves him alone from that time on. Some Navajo words and chants are included, as are notes on Navajo traditional attitudes toward coyote and toad.

Full-page pictures in mixed media hint at the landscape. Most of the illustrations are close-ups of the two characters engaged in the humorous actions of the simple text. Naturalistic animals are appropriately combined with textured and toned backgrounds and a repeated toad-like motif in "native" style that creates a somewhat unearthly impression. Grades 1 or 2-4.

Emery Bernhard, **Spotted Eagle and Black Crow: A Lakota Legend**. Illustrated by Durga Bernhard. Holiday House, 1993. 32pp.

Long ago two brothers loved the same woman. Black Crow decides to dispose of Spotted Eagle so Red Bird will marry him. He lowers Spotted Eagle down a cliff to get eagle feathers, then leaves him there to die. But Spotted Eagle prays to the Great Spirit, who has the young eagles share with him and then fly him out. There is no time for a confrontation between the brothers, because a Pawnee war party is arriving. Many die in the battle, including Black Crow. After mourning the dead, Spotted Eagle gives thanks to the Eagle nation for saving him, then marries Red Bird. Her passive role in this story, and the question of whether justice triumphed, can provoke some discussion. The author has noted the source of the story and any liberties taken.

From *Spotted Eagle & Black Crow: A Lakota Legend* by Emery Bernhard. Illustrated by Durga Bernhard. Copyright 1993. Reprinted with permission of Holiday House.

There is a decorative quality to the tints of opaque paint that produce highly stylized flat shapes. Faces have standardized lines for features and half-almond white eyes with black dot pupils. Clothes and artifacts suggest the specific tribe, while the landscape is Southwestern-ish, with cute animals peeking out from bushes and rocks. White angular areas, with patterned borders containing the simply written but lengthy text, are superimposed over the scenes. It's a rather pretty, nonrealistic vision of a story that deals with harsh reality. K or Grades 1-4.

Joseph Bruchac, **The First Strawberries: A Cherokee Story**. Illustrated by Anna Vojtech. Dial, 1993. 32pp.

Told in simple language and large print, this tale of long ago begins with a man and woman made by the Creator, married and happy. But they quarrel when the man comes home one day to find the woman picking flowers instead of cooking. She walks away so fast that he cannot catch up to say he's sorry. The sun, taking pity on him, makes first raspberries, then blueberries, then blackberries grow, but she is too angry to see them and stop to pick. Finally, when she sees strawberries, she does stop to pick some. Their sweetness reminds her of her former happiness. Her husband catches up, asks forgiveness, and receives a share of strawberries in reply. So now, for the Cherokee, eating strawberries reminds them to be kind to each other.

The text's directness is paralleled in the double-page watercolor and colored pencil illustrations. Hints of a landscape of rolling hills, a few trees, the berry bushes, all create a bucolic world. The man and woman with long black hair and dressed in buckskin move through the landscape in upright quiet, in a manner we typically call "majestic." But when she bends to pick the strawberries, her back curved to ease the picking, and when she turns to greet her approaching husband with a smile, still softly curvilinear, the loving relationship is clearly in the visualization of the forms. K-Grade 4.

Caron Lee Cohen, **The Mud Pony: A Traditional Skidi Pawnee Tale**. Illustrated by Shonto Begay. Scholastic, 1988. 32pp.

When his family and tribe move without him to follow the buffalo, a poor boy finds that the pony he has made from mud has come alive. It takes him to find his people, protects him in battle, and helps him become the chief. When the pony must finally return to Mother Earth, the chief takes off the protecting blanket and lets the rain wash the mud back to the earth. Mother Earth assures him, however, that he is still not alone. Sources of the story and the importance of the boy-hero are noted.

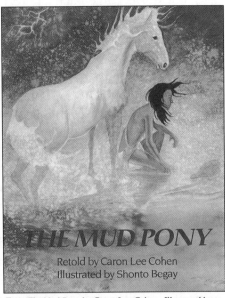

From *The Mud Pony* by Caron Lee Cohen. Illustrated by Shonto Begay. Copyright 1988. Reprinted with permission of Scholastic.

Watercolors that define people and horses, but only hint at the environment with splashy washes, create scenes that express some of the magic of the story. Most of the illustrations show the boy and his horse involved in the action of the text's adventures. Grades 1 or 2-4.

Ann Dixon, **How Raven Brought Light to People**. Illustrated by James Watts. Margaret K. McElderry/Macmillan, 1992. 32pp.

The character of Raven and the importance of light and fire to inhabitants of the colder, darker part of the continent in the Northwest occur often in tales from this area. In this simply told version of the Tlingit story told also in the books by McDermott and Shetterly below, a great chief has three wooden boxes, in which he keeps the sun, the moon, and the stars away from the people living in darkness. Raven takes the shape of a pine needle to be swallowed by the chief's daughter and is born as her child. He cries until he can get the boxes with sun and moon and release them to the heavens. But the chief is more careful of the box with the sun. Raven must fly away with it as Raven, not child, through the smoke hole the chief tries to close. The bird thus coats himself with the soot that makes him black as he brings the light of the sun to the people.

Watts has done his research, including authentic-looking artifacts in his dramatic paintings: the carved wooden boxes, chief's hat and robe, totem poles, the interior of the lodge. Several scenes depict the lakes and mountains of the Northwest. But it is the distinctly decorated objects that provide the major force of the visual narrative. Grades 1-4.

Barbara Juster Esbensen, **Ladder to the Sky: How the Gift of Healing Came to the Ojibway Nation, A Legend**. Illustrated by Helen K. Davie. Little, Brown, 1989. 32pp.

Long ago everyone was healthy, nobody died, but spirits came back and forth from Manitou in the sky to take old ones up the magic vine. A young man, once envied and shunned, goes off and up with one of the spirits. Disobeying the laws, his grandmother climbs the sacred vine after him. As punishment, Manitou sends disease and death, but also medicinal plants, along with medicine men who know how to use the plants to heal. In a brief note, the author discusses the authenticity of the source of this tale retold in simple, chant-like prose.

From *Ladder to the Sky* by Barbara Juster Esbensen. Illustrated Helen K. Davie. Copyright 1989. Reprinted with permission of Little, Brown.

Appropriately the artist borders each of the full-page watercolors with depictions of one of the medicinal plants. The scenes of Ojibway life include details of clothing, utensils, ornament, and surrounding landscape. These are naturally incorporated into dramatically composed settings that downplay color contrasts. The scene of the gift of medicinal plants from Gitchi Manitou is a particularly splendid but subtly painted vision. Grades 1 or 2-5.

Paul Goble, **Iktomi and the Berries: A Plains Indian Story**. Orchard, 1989, (paper, 1992). 32pp.

"I don't like it—that white guy, Paul Goble, is telling stories about me again..." says Iktomi on the two-page spread for the title. As the author notes, Iktomi the trickster is both clever and stupid. In this tale, he is hungry, but finds no game. He then tries for some berries in the water, which are only reflections, with predictable disaster, and giggles from the audience. In addition to the straight text, Goble has Iktomi making side comments in smaller print, with possible reader response in gray, or room for spontaneous remarks. Other chapters

From *Iktomi and the Berries* by Paul Goble. Copyright 1989. Reprinted with permission of Orchard.

in the life of Iktomi include *Iktomi and the Boulder* (Orchard, 1988) and *Iktomi and the Ducks* (Orchard, 1990)

Goble bases his picture-making on the lifestyle of the Plains peoples. The clothing, ornaments, and weapons reflect traditional customs. There's almost no landscape here, just the river, some stylized ducks, and berry bushes. The action takes place against a white background with only the three sets of text completing the pictures. In other books, *Beyond the Ridge* (Bradbury, 1989) for example, he uses the same combination of black ink outline and mostly flat watercolors, but there are full and double pages of developed settings, including regional flora and fauna, rocky mountains, and wonderfully designed clouds. Goble conveys a spiritual stillness appropriate to this story of death and afterlife. The spiritual quality is enhanced in other books like *Crow Chief* (Orchard, 1992) and *The Lost Children* (Bradbury, 1993) by repeated use of symbols and silhouettes. All his works share this quality of quiet strength, although he uses a variety of visual approaches to achieve it. K or Grades 1-4 or 5.

Ellin Greene, **The Legend of the Cranberry: A Paleo-Indian Tale**. Illustrated by Brad Sneed. Simon & Schuster, 1993. 32pp.

This legend begins in the days when the mastodons given to the People by the Great Spirit helped with the work of daily life. But when the animals began to rebel and destroy instead, all the other animals called upon the Great Spirit. He told the People to help the animals destroy the Yah-qua-whee or mastodons. A gigantic battle succeeded in this, but so many of the People and animals were killed or left hungry that the Great Spirit sent the cranberries as a symbol of peace and love, although their color and taste were reminders of the blood shed. In the spirit of peace and friendship the People shared the berries with the Pilgrims at Thanksgiving. The author's note at the end fills in both the historic and the legendary background of the story.

The watercolor double-page paintings suggest the dioramas in the natural history museums. The figures of humans and animals are depicted in a rather starkly modeled fashion, sculptural in effect; the events seem stagey, as if in frozen motion. Such drama is appropriate for telling a story of historical consequence. And such artistic license as Sneed takes is valid in order to help us get the feel of this part of human history. Perhaps as symbolic of long ago, he chooses to use subdued tones for all the scenes showing the struggles with the hairy mastodons. Grades 1-6.

Andy Gregg, **Great Rabbit and the Long-tailed Wildcat**. Illustrated by Cat Bowman Smith. Whitman, 1993. 32pp.

Long ago the wildcat was a proud creature, proudest of his long, bushy tail. This Algonquin *pourquoi* tale tells humorously how he lost it. Proud Wildcat decides to eat Great Rabbit, big, smart, and magical chief of all. Rabbit makes Wildcat chase him all day. At night Wildcat finds a wigwam with a medicine man inside, whose ears look suspiciously like Rabbit's, and of course Wildcat is tricked. The next night he is fooled by an "old woman." Finally Wildcat encounters a warrior who turns out to be Great Rabbit carrying a tomahawk to cut off his tail.

The setting of this essentially two-character play is a snowy, woodsy place, including several interior scenes where Great Rabbit assumes human form. Bits of architecture, masks, and robes add the flavor of the specific region. Opaque gouache paints, vigorously applied, fill the pages with naturalistic but decidedly comic representations. Each text page is bordered with decorative, mostly geometric designs in colors to complement those in the facing illustrations. Grades K-4.

From *Great Rabbit and the Long-tailed Wildcat* by Andy Gregg. Illustrated by Cat Bowman Smith. Copyright 1993. Reprinted with permission of Whitman.

L. Michael Kershen, **Why Buffalo Roam**. Illustrated by Monica Hansen. Stemmer House, 1993. 32pp.

A ten-year-old student in Oklahoma wrote this story as an assignment after a unit on Native American peoples. He chose to study and write about the Comanche. In one or two sentences per page, he tells how Whitewolf's prayers to the Spirit for relief from famine are answered. Whitewolf must offer his most precious thing. When all else is rejected, he is ready to sacrifice his son. Spirit, seeing his loyalty, gives the buffalo to him and his people.

The artist, who has exhibited her work at American Indian art shows, paints a few Comanche artifacts, an isolated cloud, a skeleton, but mainly Whitewolf in his wolfskin, all isolated on a textured purple page opposite the white page of text. The stark pictures reflect the minimal text of the story. K-Grade 5.

Jonathan London with Larry Pinola, **Fire Race: A Karuk Coyote Tale About How Fire Came to the People**. Illustrated by Sylvia Long. Chronicle, 1993. 40pp.

Wise Old Coyote devises a plan to steal fire from the Yellow Jacket sisters for the cold and miserable animal people. When he tricks the sisters and runs away with fire, they are in close pursuit. As planned, each animal in turn picks up the fire as the other flags: eagle, mountain lion, fox, bear, worm, turtle, and finally frog, who

From *Fire Race* by Jonathon London. Illustrated by Sylvia Long. Copyright 1993. Reprinted with permission of Chronicle.

swallows it until the Yellow Jackets tire of waiting for him to give it back and go home. When frog spits the remaining hot coal into the willow roots, which swallow it, the animals fear all is lost, until Coyote shows them how to coax fire from willow sticks over dry moss. Then they have fire forever as needed. In addition to the simply but excitingly told story, there is an afterword about stories and storytelling in his tribe by Karuk Julian Lang, and a useful bibliography.

The double-page scenes first realistically depict in ink and watercolors the northern California landscape with the shivering animal people. Later pictures show the adventures in detailed close-ups and several multiple images, like the tumbling of Coyote through the snow. The text is integrated in panels at the tops or bottoms of the pages, separated with linear borders that are displayed in the endpapers, on Coyote's cap, and on the objects in the Yellow Jackets' house. Long vividly depicts the characters in action. Grades 1 or 2-5.

Rafe Martin, **The Boy Who Lived With the Seals**. Illustrated by David Shannon. Putnam, 1993. 32pp.

Legends of seal-children abound in many cultures. In this version of a Chinook legend, a young boy wanders off along the river and cannot be found. A few years later, the People among whom he had lived hear of a boy seen with seals on an island in the river. It turns out to be the missing boy, who is brought back to his delighted parents. He must be taught to walk and talk again, but he carves wonderful canoes, paddles, bows and arrows, and tells tales of life under the sea. Whenever the family goes out on the water, the boy hears the seals and tries to rejoin them. One day he breaks free, waves goodbye and is gone. His parents leave his carving tools in a box in the water for him. Every year when they return to that place, a beautiful new canoe and paddle await them. Martin adds a note about the Chinook people and how he came to this story.

The art forms of the Chinook dominate the naturalistic pictures. The apparel is depicted, but mainly the carved boxes and canoes plus a wonderfully imaginative undersea structure display the characteristic designs of the region. The scenes are dramatically lighted, mixing close-ups, including a stunner of the boy with a fish in his mouth, with wide-angle views. Opaque acrylic paints model all forms, even the waves and clouds. There are touches reminiscent of the romantic realism of N. C. Wyeth's illustrated classics. K-Grade 4.

___, **The Rough-Face Girl**. Illustrated by David Shannon. Putnam, 1992. 32pp.

This Cinderella tale, noted by the author as an Algonquin Indian story, concerns two cruel older sisters and the youngest, called Rough-Face, who has become burnt and scarred from her sisters' mistreatment. In their village, in a separated, huge dwelling, lives an Invisible Being and his sister. Since he is supposed to be rich and handsome, the two cruel sisters, dressed in their best, try to marry him. But they have to have seen him first. Questions from his sister soon prove that they have not. Then Rough-Face girl goes to the Invisible Being, for she says she has seen his face everywhere. Her father has nothing left to give her, so she dresses in what she can find. And of course she becomes beautiful, marries, and lives happily ever after. The text is lengthy but not difficult.

Using the same techniques and styles found in the paintings that illustrate *The Boy Who Lived With the Seals* by the same team, described above,

Shannon's many close-ups and all scenes approach the melodramatic. The illustrations here also include many details of landscape, costume and artifacts. There has been some argument about the mixing of wigwams and tipis and other details of authenticity, but the story receives the romantic visualization it deserves. Grades 1 or 2-6.

Gerald McDermott, **Arrow to the Sun: A Pueblo Indian Tale**. Viking, 1974. 42pp.

When Boy seeks his father, he is shot as an "arrow to the sun," who tells him he must prove to be his child by passing through the Kivas of Lions, Serpents, Bees, and Lightening. Boy does this all, emerging from the Kiva of Lightning filled with the power of the sun, which his father allows him to bring back to the people of the pueblo. This simply told tale has the universal hero quest and search-for-the-power-of-light theme that occur in so many cultures.

The geometry of Pueblo architecture is McDermott's logical base for building all shapes using a highly abstracted style: rectangles for males, more rounded shapes for females. As is typical in McDermott's illustrations, the opaque gouache and ink colors are intense, used for fullest emotional impact, while the invented symbols are organized to emphasize action. Double pages, often without any text, tell this mythic tale in ways that invite, even demand, our involvement. K-Grade 4.

___, **Raven: A Trickster Tale from the Pacific Northwest**. Harcourt Brace, 1993. 32pp.

Raven, the culture hero of many moods and powers, here searches for light for the men and women of the world who live in darkness. He finds it at Sky Chief's house. Raven transforms himself into Sky Chief's grandchild, tricks the chief into giving him the ball of the sun, then turns back into Raven to bring it to the people. After notes on Raven as a character and an art motif, we have a simply told version of the story we saw by Dixon above and will see again told by Shetterly below.

These large double pages are designed more naturalistically than those in his *Arrow to the Sun* above. McDermott, using mixed media, begins with a misty dark landscape and concludes with a bright one illuminated by the liberated sun. Classical decorative forms, clean-cut shapes like those in the brilliant reds and greens on Raven's body, and more muted in the wood carvings and the clothing of Sky Chief's family, all are set against solid color backgrounds. McDermott's interpretations create great eye appeal as they project the quality of such art forms in the life of the people of the Pacific Northwest. K-Grade 4.

Howard Norman, **Who-Paddled-Backward-With-Trout**. Illustrated by Ed Young. Joy Street/Little, Brown, 1987. 32pp.

A young Cree boy who always seems to be bumping into things acquires the name of "Trout-With-Flattened-Nose." When he grows older, he is not happy with this name, so he seeks another. He must earn it, however, and then ask permission of the old man who suggested the name he has. The old man is now a trout, so the boy paddles out into the lake seeking him, and hoping for a new name as a paddler. But beavers steal his paddle. A trout offers to tow him, and when the fish goes toward the rocks, the boy grabs him and uses him to paddle back and away. So he earns not the name he desired, but the title name instead. The author notes the source of this humorous but lengthy story.

Young's black silhouettes capture the characteristics of the animals, fish and people in a uniquely animated fashion. Some almost fill the double pages with intricate, lacy shapes, like that of the owls sleeping in a moon-dappled tree, while others use only a part, like the boy's fight with the beaver. A thin blue border around all pages, frequently broken by the active illustrations, provides a dimensional frame of reference. Grades 1 or 2-5.

From *Who-Paddled-Backward-With-Trout* by Howard Norman. Illustrated by Ed Young. Copyright 1987. Reprinted with permission of Little, Brown.

Jamie Oliviero, **The Fish Skin**. Illustrated by Brent Morrison. Hyperion, 1993. 40pp.

When a young boy realizes that the heat and drought from the unremitting sun will soon cause his grandmother and others to die, he decides to ask the Great Spirit who lives on the other side of the camp for rain. To help the brave boy, the Great Spirit leaves him a fish skin, which gives him fish powers when he puts it on. With the aid of Cloud and with all the water he swallows as a fish, the boy makes it rain. The simply told original story carries the magic of legend.

Intense colors, oranges and yellows, purples and blues, are exploited for strong emotional impressions in the complexly designed double pages. Objects overlap one another in scenes of vigorous action, like that of a leaping fish shown against a sun with wiggling rays. Humans tend to be crudely pictured when compared with the depiction of the animals, while the forest environment is suggested by flat backdrops of greenery. K-Grade 4.

Teri Sloat, **The Eye of the Needle**. Based on a Yupik tale as told by Betty Huffman. Dutton, 1990. 32pp.

Long ago, the legend says, Little Amik and his grandmother were running out of food in their hut by the sea. She feels he is old enough to be sent out to hunt food. Amik swallows ever larger fish, and walrus up to whale, until he is finally no longer hungry, but he has saved nothing for grandmother. He returns tired, but too large now to squeeze through the smoke hole, until she uses her magic needle. Then in he pops, and out pops all he swallowed, making enough for a fine feast for both.

The good humor of the telling is neatly illustrated with color pencil pictures of Amik's gustatory adventures. The sod hut, the seacoast, birds, and sea creatures are depicted naturalistically in large and small scenes, several when there are action sequences. The concluding double-page spreads are especially joyful when Amik's catch gushes out, the lines of text flow with the fish and the hut's utensils, and even a sailing ship from the whale's mouth. K or Grades 1-4 or 5.

Susan Hand Shetterly, **Raven's Light: A Myth from the People of the Northwest Coast**. Illustrated by Robert Shetterly. Atheneum, 1991. 32pp.

Raven here is first responsible for creating the land amid the sea, and then all the creatures. But the only light is from the stars. Beyond the sky Raven sees the Kingdom of Day. He changes into a piece of cedar frond in the water drunk by the chief's daughter, and so is born as her child. He cries so much to play with the bright ball of Day that the chief allows it, giving him the opportunity to change back into Raven and carry it away. But in this more detailed version of the story told above by both Ann Dixon and Gerald McDermott, the people don't want Day. One young girl throws him a fish, so setting free the moon and the sun.

The opening scenes of Raven in the dark world he creates and fills with trees and animals are painted to emphasize the gloomy atmosphere. Then the mood changes, as scenes of people wearing carved masks and decorated robes act out the adventures in the Kingdom of Light. Ultimately the return to the dark is pictured dramatically when the girl holds the light in the basket and uses it as a spotlight. This artist's more enigmatic vision reflects a more powerful and mysterious Raven. Grades 1 or 2-5.

William Toye, **The Loon's Necklace**. Illustrated by Elizabeth Cleaver. Oxford University Press, paper, 1977. 24pp.

This Tsimshian legend from Canada tells of a blind old man who has been deprived of the meat he deserved by an old hag. He goes to Loon, a wise and magical bird, asking to be able to see again so he can feed his family. Loon magically restores his sight. In gratitude, he tosses Loon his shell necklace, the pieces of which come to decorate Loon's back from this time. When the old man returns home, the hag comes seeking shelter from a storm. When she is turned away, she turns herself into an owl to screech and annoy them. The family leaves, but the old man can now see so they do not go hungry.

The spare quality of the telling is matched by the illustrations achieved simply with collage elements. Characters are formed with colored shapes and black woodcut-like interior details. Other objects like trees, canoe, and Loon are pictured in the same way. They are set against textured and tan papers representing mountains and water. The sense of the Pacific Northwest is well expressed. Grades 2-4.

Nancy Van Laan, reteller, **Buffalo Dance: A Blackfoot Legend**. Illustrated by Beatriz Vidal. Little, Brown, 1993. 32pp.

This legend goes back generations, telling of a time when the buffalo refused to be caught. To save her people from hunger, a woman promises to marry one of them, and is taken away by him. When her father comes to find her, he is trampled by the buffalo. With the help of a magical magpie, she reassembles his body, prays, and brings him back to life. Impressed by her feat, the buffalo teach her and her father their dance and song. The tribe can repeat this each year after the hunt so the buffalo will return. Thus the origin of the Blackfoot Buffalo Dance is explained. An introduction offers further information, and a glossary is included.

Vidal incorporates some pictograph symbols along the bottom of the text pages, and decorative devices of the Blackfoot down the sides to supplement her personal interpretation of the story. Her illustrations, using what appears to be colored pencils, are full-page scenes depicting native plants, landscapes, and the Blackfoot people with, of course, lots of buffalo. Hers is a stripped-down naturalism that focuses on action and detail rather than character development. The only double-page picture is a stunning one showing the heroine and her father in the center of a circle of dancing buffalo. There is a sense of magic here, and a proper expression of mythic significance in all the illustrations. Grades 2-5 or 6.

Jane Yolen, **Sky Dogs**. Illustrated by Barry Moser. Harcourt Brace, 1990. 32pp.

Drawing on several stories and legends of the Blackfeet people as described in her notes, Yolen has constructed a story as told by an old man, explaining why he is called He-Who-Loves-Horses. He tells of how long ago, when his people had to walk everywhere and they first saw horses. They called them Sky Dogs, gifts from the Blackfoot creator figure, the Old Man. A woman who came with the horses married the father of the old narrator, and taught him how to care for these new creatures.

Moser's transparent watercolors illustrate the text's actions in double pages that depict the vastness of the plains under a relentless sun. He uses oval-framed portraits and rectangular-shaped illustrations, all saturated with the browns and yellows of that region. Realistic pictures that show the blades of grass and the curly texture of a fur hat are also visions of a vanished people as conceived by a skillful and sensitive artist. Grades 1-4.

Robert Andrew Parker has illustrated two books of interest here. *The Woman Who Fell from the Sky: The Iroquois Story of Creation* retold by John Bierhorst (Morrow, 1993) makes an interesting comparison with other creation stories. *The Trees Stand Shining: Poetry of the North American Indian*, selected by Hettie Jones (Dial, 1971) makes useful supplementary reading. In both books watery pigments and thin scratchy ink lines create impressions of places and people in action. The bits of costumes are not specific enough for visual cultural information.

The art in *Dancing Teepees: Poems of American Indian Youth*, selected by Virginia Driving Hawk Sneve (Holiday House, 1989) and illustrated by Stephen Gammell, offers more cultural information. Gammell's figures and objects in mixed media include decorations based on Indian fabrics, beadwork, painted petroglyphs, and specific objects such as Kachina dolls and Navaho sand paintings, all finely and respectfully rendered.

Native American Life Today

Peter Cumming, **Out on the Ice in the Middle of the Bay**. Illustrated by Alice Priestley. Annick Press, hardback and paper, 1993. 32pp.

Leah lives where ice and snow cover the land by November. One day as the sun is setting, while her mother is away and her father naps, Leah goes exploring. On the other side of the iceberg in the bay, while his mother sleeps, Baby Nanook polar bear also goes exploring. While her father and his mother wake and begin frantic searching, girl and polar bear meet at the iceberg and, amazingly, cuddle together. Then his mother and her father meet; luckily both paw and gun miss their targets. Reunited with their children, the parents back away from confrontation. Leah goes happily home to end this simple tale of wonder written by a resident of Canada's eastern Arctic.

 Priestly's color pencils create a visual tone poem, a blurry reaffirmation of the innocence of all of nature's young. Scenes are lighted by the sky-blue pinks of the near-polar North. The people are properly in parkas, the landscape suitably vast, and the iceberg handsomely sculptured. K-Grade 4.

Nancy White Carlstrom, **Northern Lullaby**. Illustrated by Leo and Diane Dillon. Philomel, 1992. 28pp.

This simple lullaby says "Goodnight" to the aspects of nature in an Alaska winter, addressing them as benign relatives, like "Great Moose Uncle" and "Auntie Willow," all around the sleeping child.

 Airbrush creates human and anthropomorphic portraits that gleam in the magic frozen Arctic night. Curves dominate as if to suggest the soft mounding of snow. Geometric designs complement the large, smooth areas of the involved large scenes. The sky is jet black with symbolic square, light blue stars. Endpapers include a decorated border with hanging multicolored tassels. This is visual poetry designed to partner the lullaby. K-Grade 2.

Fiona French, **The Magic Vase**. Oxford University Press, 1990. 32pp.

French's parable concerns a wealthy dealer of antique pots and vases, who has amassed the second-best collection in the world. He hears that a valuable vase has been found, one to make his collection the best, right in the town where he was born. When he arrives there, Maria the potter, who sees how greedy he has become, makes a magic vase with the help of a snake. This reminds him of the true value of such things; that after he dies his collection will simply belong to someone else. After the magic vase speaks to him he feels he has nothing, until Maria gives him a small pot for his collection. He returns to it a wiser man.

 The Southwest desert, Pueblo country, with its yellow-browns and characteristic buildings, is painted in scenes to fill the large double pages. The dealer, a sharp dresser with slick black hair and curling mustache, seems out of the 1930s. Maria is dressed in patterned blouse and skirt with traditional silver necklace. Patterns reflecting tradition fill the pots, clothing, and creatures from the changing vase. The magic is illustrated in boldly inventive pictures that show the pot's growth and change. Grades 1 or 2-5.

Barbara M. Joosse, **Mama, Do You Love Me?** Illustrated by Barbara Lavallee. Chronicle, 1991. 28pp.

by Barbara M. Joosse   illustrated by Barbara Lavallee

In answer to the universal question asked in the title, and those that follow, Mama uses the world of nature around and the traditional objects of an Arctic home to reassure her child that her love is there "forever and always," no matter what the questioner might do or turn into. Questions and answers are simple, and rhythmically reassuring.

From *Mama, Do You Love Me?* by Barbara M. Joosse. Illustrated by Barbara Lavallee. Copyright 1991. Reprinted with permission of Chronicle.

Visualizing the loving relationship with hugs and other appropriate gestures, the artist creates mother and daughter figures who, page by page, keep changing costumes. They are mainly set against a bare white background that shows off the dress patterns and fancifully pictured animals of the verbal game. Watercolors and color pencils create engaging personalities as well as providing local details of outdoor gear, sealskin boat (*umiak*), sled, and a series of circular masks based on traditional models, including four large ones on the endpapers. An added bonus are two pages of information on the Inuit and the items and creatures of the story. Grades K-3.

Michael Arvaarluk Kusugak, **Hide and Sneak**. Illustrated by Vladyana Krykorka. Annick Press, hardback and paper, 1992. 32pp.

In this contemporary story, Allashua meets a character from traditional tales when she plays hide-and-seek, a game at which she's not very good. Fortunately the Ijiraq she encounters who, her mother warns her, may hide her so no one will ever find her, is not very good at the game either. Allashua is frequently distracted by butterflies, fish, birds, and other animals. When the Ijiraq offers to hide her, she thinks her mother was wrong, and goes to a cave with him. But then he won't let her out. Luckily she outstares the shy creature, but still is lost. This is when she finds out what the strange stone man-like constructions called *inuksugaqs* are for: to help you find your way home.

Some magic still works. The vital stone sculpture is pictured significantly in an early scene at the water's edge and on the cover. Watercolors create windswept cloudy skies and clear waters. Mixed media detail the flowery fields, Allashua's family, and the mythical sprite. Each painted scene is bordered with a band of black rubbings of objects relating to the scene. Also included are a few words written in Inuit but not translated. Grades 1 or 2-5.

Nancy Luen, **Nessa's Fish**. Illustrated by Neil Waldman. Atheneum, 1992. 32pp.

In the Arctic of today, Nessa and her grandmother have caught fish for themselves and everyone in camp. But grandmother becomes ill. Many animals come after the fish during the long day while grandmother rests. Remembering what her parents have taught her, Nessa protects herself and grandmother along with the fish until rescued.

Double pages are designed with a thin rectangle on the left edge and a large rectangle on the right page. The watercolor illustrations sweep from the left edge to the right edge, missing only the small section of simple text, as if to emphasize the vastness of the Arctic ice fields, with undulating bands of pastel colors breaking out of thin black frames on left and right. Nessa and her family are dressed in parkas. The sequence of pictures, clouds, fish, are all neatly arranged. K or Grades 1-4.

George Ella Lyon, **Dreamplace**. Illustrated by Peter Catalanotto. Orchard, 1993. 32pp.

Author and illustrator take us with a group of tourists to visit the pueblo where once the Anasazi lived. The life of long ago is pictured and described in spare, simple, poetic prose. We also see what the pueblo looks like now.

The watercolors picture the imagined life in double-page illustrations with fuzzy edges to suggest the dreaminess of it all. The buildings of the city and the people going about routine tasks are painted with a parallel naturalistic fuzziness in a pinkish golden light. The shift from and return to the young tourist's world is achieved smoothly. The final textless page showing a modern-day girl peeking into a darkened room is symbolic of the attractive mystery of the Anasazi culture. K or Grades 1-4.

From *Dreamplace* by George Ella Lyon. Illustrated by Peter Catalanotto. Copyright 1993. Reprinted with permission of Orchard.

Jean Rogers, **Runaway Mittens**. Illustrated by Rie Munoz. Greenwillow, 1988. 24pp.

In this simple story of a family in Alaska today, young Pica has a problem common to many young children: the wonderful red mittens his grandmother knitted for him keep disappearing. They "run away," and he and his family have to track them down each time. Where they finally end up, as Spring luckily nears, makes for a satisfying end.

Details of Pica's home life, his village, his pregnant sled dog, all are pictured simply in watercolors against the bare white page. The artist treats objects decoratively. The night skies are like twisted skeins of dark blue yarn, snowflakes are white dots, clothing is sculptured form, faces have black-dot eyes and circular red cheeks. All the animated pictures share the light fun of the story. K-Grade 2.

Background Books

Tundra Books in Montreal is publishing a series of heavily texted 24-page re-creations of native legends by C. J. Taylor, illustrated by the Mohawk artist with full-color paintings that give a sense of the natural setting. They include *How Two-Feather Was Saved from Loneliness: An Abenaki Legend* (1990), *The Ghost and Lone Warrior* (1991), and *Little Water and the Gift of the Animals: A Seneca Legend* (1992)

    Tundra is also publishing a series about native dwellings by Bonnie Shemie. All are 24 pages with color illustrations. They include *Houses of Bark: Tipi, Wigwam and Longhouse* (1990) and *Houses of Wood* (1992)

    Who Speaks for Wolf: As Told to Turtle Woman Singing by her Father, Sharp-eyed Hawk is a 51-page Native American Learning Story by Paula Underwood Spencer (Tribe Two Press, paper, 1991) with the cadence of a chant, illustrated with detailed realistic paintings and drawings by Frank Howell.

    Claire Rudolf Murphy's *The Prince and the Salmon People* (Rizzoli, 1993) illustrated by Duane Pasco with Northwest Coast Art from Museum Collections offers a 48-page retelling of a legend with visual materials to bring the art to life.

Photoessays with much valuable information include:

George Ancona, **Powwow**. Harcourt Brace, hardback and paper, 1993. 48pp.

Diane Hoyt-Goldsmith, **Cherokee Summer**. 1993.
___, **Pueblo Storyteller**. 1991.
___, **Totem Pole**. 1990. All illustrated by photographs by Lawrence Migdale. All Holiday House.

    In the Fall of 1993 the Smithsonian is publishing **Indian Country**, "a comprehensive history of America's Indians from the Indian point of view" to be illustrated with over 500 full-color maps, charts, photos, and reproductions.
    For black and white photographs and reproductions of Native American art for reference, see Shirley Glubok's series for children including **The Art of the Plains Indians**, **The Art of the Southeastern Indians**, **The Art of the Southwest Indians**, and **The Art of the Northwest Coast Indians**, all published by Macmillan.

Notes

Section 8

Europe and the European Immigrant Experience

We have not tried to deal with the various cultures of Europe as expressed in picture books for several reasons. First of all, a European background is still the most common one for a majority of Americans. Perhaps because of this, the myths and legends of Aesop, those collected by the Grimm brothers, and those others from this area have long been available for children in many versions, including picture books. An entire book could be compiled analyzing these. Distinctive crafts, architecture, and costume have all but disappeared from European daily life. Cultures there are tending to become transnational, despite the current rise of some ethnic conflicts. Finally, because they are part of the majority, children with this background do not seem to have such a strong need for self-esteem building.

For a sampling, however, we have selected some books from an area from which large numbers of immigrants are still arriving, one which still has distinctive art and artifacts to picture, and some less-known tales to tell. That area is the former Soviet Union.

We also include here some picture book explorations of the experiences of the large numbers of European immigrants who arrived around the turn of the century. While some of these are time and place-specific, some surely have implications about all immigrants to impart to children.

Original Tales and Folk Tales of the Past from the Former Soviet Union

Katya Arnold, **Baba Yaga: A Russian Folk Tale**. North-South, 1993. 28pp.

The author here retells one of the many stories about Baba Yaga, an important character of Russian folklore less known in America, as she reminds us in her informative notes. Tishka, the magically created son of an old couple, goes fishing every day until called back by his mother. He has been warned about Baba Yaga, the witch who snatches and eats children, but is fooled when she disguises her voice. Tishka is taken to her house, where her daughter tries to put him in the oven. He fools her as Gretel did her witch, then teases Baba Yaga when she returns. When almost captured, he is saved by a gosling flying by. Both are welcomed back by his happy parents.

A folk tale takes on folksy overtones when illustrated by folk art-style pictures. Here crude 17th-century woodcuts are the basis for pictures with rough-hewn black outlines filled in with opaque gouache colors. Thin bands of varying colors act as frames around all sizes of illustrations, from three-on-a-page sequential vignettes to double-page scenes so aggressively drawn that they burst their borders. Grotesquely naturalistic, the pictures move the story at a brisk pace. But there are such details as the samovar, costumes, Baba Yaga's chicken-footed house, outdoor oven, to remind us of the place and time. The decorative patchwork end-papers help set us up for this rough-and-ready depiction. Grades 2-5.

Carolyn Croll, **The Little Snowgirl: An Old Russian Tale**. Putnam, 1989. 32pp.

Another old couple who have always wanted a child enjoy one they have made from snow, which comes to life. But she must stay outside. By Christmas Eve, her mother Caterina cannot bear to let her sleep in the snow, so she brings her inside where Babouschka the bringer of gifts can find her. But in the morning she is gone. They weep, until they hear their Snowgirl laugh. Babouschka has given her what she wanted most, life as their real child.

Details from some undefined period of "old Russian" history fill the stage-like scenes, settings that suggest the influence of Tomie de Paola's "creative direction." Figures are painted to emphasize their solidity, features simplified to strengthen the emotional impact of gestures and expressions. Clothing, interiors with samovar, religious icons, cookies and wood carvings, all add to the sense of Russia. The illustrations vary from a double-page spread to multiple small boxes showing action, with the text exploiting the white spaces above or below the pictures. Grades 1-4.

Eric A. Kimmel, **Baba Yaga: A Russian Folktale**. Illustrated by Megan Lloyd. Holiday House, 1991. 32pp.

Another alternative look at Baba Yaga, this time in a variation of the traditional story of the two daughters, one lazy and spoiled by her mother, the other good and pretty, except this one has a horn growing from her forehead. When her father leaves on a trip, her stepmother makes Marina a Cinderella-like servant. Finally the stepmother sends her into the woods to Baba Yaga. A friendly frog gives the frightened girl the advice she will need to deal with the hazards the witch presents when Marina arrives at her house requesting the removal of her horn. The cat that Marina cares for tells her what else she will need to escape

From *Baba Yaga: A Russian Folktale* by Eric A. Kimmel. Illustrated by Megan Lloyd. Copyright 1991. Reprinted with permission of Holiday House.

and return to her loving father. When he turns the stepmother and her daughter out, the latter goes to see Baba Yaga and receives the justice she deserves in this action-packed, humorous adventure.

The tidy detailed ink-and-watercolor paintings in the black frames tend to underplay the range of human emotions in the narrative. There are many details of dress, architecture, and landscape that suggest, if not define, historic eastern Europe. Characters are made to act for smiles even when they're up to no good. Pictures, large and small, are complete scenes that, in sequence, are quite cinematographic in their storytelling effects. K-Grade 4.

Eric A. Kimmel, **Bearhead: A Russian Folktale**. Illustrated by Charles Mikolaycak. Holiday House, 1991. 32pp.

Found and raised as their own by a peasant couple, Bearhead has a human body, bear's head and strength, and love and obedience for his "parents." When Hexaba, the witch who rules the area, summons the father to serve her, Bearhead goes in his stead. He infuriates the witch by following her instructions literally, with humorous but disastrous results. Sent by her to collect gold from the goblin of the lake, he tricks the goblin, then the witch. But when he brings the gold to his parents, he feels the call to return to "his own people" in the forest. In his author's note, Kimmel tells how he has changed the hero and villain from tradition.

From *Bearhead: A Russian Folktale* by Eric A. Kimmel. Illustrated by Charles Mikolaycak. Copyright 1991. Reprinted with permission of Holiday House.

The artist creates individuals and sets them in fully detailed scenes using specifics of clothing, household objects, and landscapes to clue us into time and place. In this case it is early 20th-century Russia, in both upper and lower class homes, as seen in details like the telephone, the samovar, the houses and furniture. Large double pages are designed to hold both the elaborately complex watercolor and pencil paintings, with thin red frames, and the lengthy text. The tongue-in-cheek question of Bearhead's intelligence is played for full visually subtle effect, while Madame Hexaba's personality is a sheer delight. Grades 1 or 2-5.

Carole Kismaric, **The Rumor of Pavel and Paali: A Ukrainian Folktale**. Illustrated by Charles Mikolaycak Harper, 1988. 32pp.

This text is long for a picture book; it is also full of greed, cruelty, and wickedness before good finally triumphs. Evil Pavel takes everything from his good twin brother Paali, even his eyes. Blind Paali, lost in the Great Forest, hears the evil spirits' secrets. He uses these to regain his sight, help the other villagers, and cure the tsar's daughter. He goes home well and wealthy. Pavel, hoping to gain from Paali's experience, also goes to the forest. But the evil spirits find and take him away.

The double-page illustrations are crowded with visual information relating to a Ukrainian 19th century life style (with some Russian additions), including clothing, buildings, fabrics and patterns, wagons, even the wooden rake. Space is also taken by the black-bordered blocks of text that incorporate panels of patterned textiles. The jumbled look of crowd scenes, or of others showing the accumulation of Paali's goods, adds to the melodramatic presentation of this bittersweet legend. The realism of gestures and facial features, as when Paali is sitting as a blind beggar in the town square, enhances the humanistic message. Grades 2-6.

Charles Mikolaycak, **Babushka: An Old Russian Folktale**. Holiday House, hardback and paper, 1984. 32pp.

This classic concerns the peasant woman who is too busy cleaning to join the Wise Men the night they stop on their way to see the Baby Jesus. By the time she is ready, she is too late to catch up with them. Over the years she has continued to search, leaving the holiday gifts for children throughout the world.

Details of the inside and outside of Babushka's log house, her fringed shawl and tightly wound hair, all spell Russia of a time past. In later illustrations, designed as vignettes and larger scenes, glimpses of other clues

From *Babushka* by Charles Mikolaycak. Copyright 1984. Reprinted with permission of Holiday House.

such as church domes, carriages, storefronts, calendars, depict the passing years of her endless searching. Less dramatically lit than some of his other illustrations, these still bear Mikolaycak's brand of romantic realism, a style that delivers large amounts of information in imaginatively composed tableaux. The attractive young woman on the jacket is a contrast to the old women we associate with "babushka," as in the Polacco story below. Grades 1 or 2-4.

Patricia Polacco, **Babushka Baba Yaga**. Philomel, 1993. 32pp.

Polacco takes the traditionally wicked witch of Russian folklore, Baba Yaga, and builds a new story around her. This Baba Yaga, "the last of her kind," is alone, lonely, jealous of the babushkas, or grandmothers, she sees, longing to have a grandchild of her own. One day she steals some grandmother-type clothes, cleans herself up, and finds a child whose mother needs a babushka to care for him while she works. All is well until tales about Baba Yaga's wickedness make her fear discovery. She leaves, "never to return," until the day when wolves are about to attack her beloved child. Then Baba Yaga must reveal herself to save him. The child recognizes and still loves her as his babushka. Acceptance by the rest of the people follows.

Patterned fabrics dominate these double pages in the multiple skirts, vests, blouses and scarves worn by the old women, even the tablecloths and rugs are featured parts of the environment that create a sense of place. Pencil drawings depict a gaggle of babushkas gossiping and playing with grandchildren. Watercolors add the blues and oranges. Birch trees, forest animals, fairy creatures, onion dome churches, peak-roofed houses, a samovar, are all added naturalistically. Polacco shows us the witch's visual conversion in ways to convince us of the spiritual change. Grade 1 or 2-5.

___, **Rechenka's Eggs**. Philomel, 1988. 32pp.

In another original folk-type tale, a Babushka living in the country is famous for her Ukrainian style painted Easter eggs. One winter day she rescues a wounded goose whom she names Rechenka. When the goose blunders into and breaks the eggs Babushka has been painstakingly preparing to sell at the Easter festival, Rechenka begins to lay brilliantly colored eggs, as a repayment. These miracles Babushka takes to the festival, to win the prize. When she returns home, Rechenka has flown away with the other geese, but left a wonderful surprise.

Traditional patterns on the eggs compete with those on clothes and quilts. Even the goose's feathers are treated as overlapping patterns. Along with costumes and icons, the rendering of old brown stave churches and of course, St. Basil's in Moskva, set the place. White backgrounds emphasize the sensitive pencil drawings and decorative watercolors. Her depiction of gestures and facial features convince us of the artist's love for her characters. K or Grades 1-4.

Elsa Okon Rael's *Marushka's Egg* (Four Winds, 1993) is really too long for a picture book, but its story includes Baba Yaga and painted eggs. Joanna Wezyk's opaque paintings with flowered borders and spattered surfaces include many details from eastern Europe such as samovar, stove, and costumes. Story and illustrations both make interesting comparisons with the other books here.

Sally Scott, **The Three Wonderful Beggars**. Greenwillow, 1987. 32pp.

This adaptation of the Andrew Lang version of a Russian folktale is long on words but not complex. Young Anna persuades her rich but hard-hearted father Mark to allow three old men to sleep in their loft. When she tells her father that they have decided to give a child called Vassili his riches, Mark takes Vassili and hurls him over a cliff. The child is found, so Mark puts him to sea in a barrel. Monks find Vassili and raise him. When Mark encounters Vassili again, he sends the young man to his house with a note saying he should be killed. But the beggars intervene, having Vassili marry young Anna instead. Finally Mark sends Vassili to the Serpent King, who answers riddles that enrich Vassili and entrap Mark.

The setting is formal, with thin-framed paintings and facing text pages. The pictures are detailed in the manner of miniatures with each stone and bit of bark clearly defined. Scenes include finely rendered regional buildings, splendid fabrics, period costumes. These are presented as frozen tableaux to emphasize the timeless nature of this moral legend. The front and rear cover paintings of the three beggars in the snow properly introduce and conclude the story. Grades 1 or 2-5.

Elizabeth Winthrop, **Vasilissa the Beautiful**. Illustrated by Alexander Koshkin. HarperCollins, 1991. 40pp.

In this heavily worded tale, lovely Vasilissa's story begins like Cinderella's. When her father leaves on a trip, her wicked stepmother sends her into the forest where Baba Yaga lives, hoping the witch will eat her when she asks for a light. With only the talking doll her mother had left to help, Vasilissa works for the witch. She finally brings back a burning skull which consumes her wicked stepmother and sister. Then with the help of the doll she weaves a shirt for the tsar so fine that he feels he must meet her, falls in love, and marries her. The author adds notes about the story.

Seventeenth-century Russia is the stated setting, so the costumes of the tsar's company and the merchant's womenfolk are the stuff of opera, sumptuously layered and ornamented. In nine large paintings, three full-page and six double-page, we are treated to a finely wrought series of portraits of a resolute heroine with a few details of daily life, a Baba Yaga of doubtless evil, and even glimpses of onion-domed churches and distant sailing ships. But these are illustrations of only a portion of the story. They offer local color, atmospheric landscapes, and emotions proper for fairy tales. Grades 1 or 2-4

Ernest Small's *Baba Yaga* (Houghton Mifflin, 1966, paper 1992) gives us another extensive version of the witch's story, not really a picture book but enlivened by Blair Lent's distinctive woodcut-ish linear shapes, stained here and there with color. Typical Russian buildings and artifacts add specific ethnic color, making this useful for comparisons.

John Cech offers another long background story that includes the traditional Snowflake and Grandfather Frost of the Russian holiday season in *First Snow, Magic Snow* (Four Winds, 1992). Sharon McGinley's illustrations are stylized and prettified, but full of ethnic costumes and patterns.

More interesting background can be found in Michael McCurdy's *The Devils Who Learned to Be Good* (Joy Street/Little, Brown, 1987), too wordy to be a picture book but a good Russian story with great engraving illustrations including touches of architecture and uniforms.

J. Patrick Lewis's *The Tsar & the Amazing Cow* (Dial, 1988) is another long, not really picture-book story. Friso Henstra's ink drawings with pale watercolors create a rural Russia with barns, carts, village houses and costumes. The scene of the tsar growing younger and going back five generations with costume changes is special.

The European Immigrant Experience

Elisa Bartone, **Peppe the Lamplighter**. Illustrated by Ted Lewin. Lothrop, 1993. 32pp.

The author has based the story loosely on one told about her grandfather, using the names of his real family and eight sisters. Since his mother is dead and his father ill, Peppe tries to find work to earn some money in Little Italy, where Italian immigrants lived in New York City at the turn of the century. No one will hire him until the lamplighter, who lights the gas lights in the street in the days before electricity, asks Peppe to do his job while he goes back to Italy. At first Peppe enjoys the work, but his father's disapproval of it as not important depresses him. One night he simply doesn't light the lamps. That same night, his littlest sister has not come home. Peppe's father finally admits that the job is important, that everyone needs the lamps lit. Peppe lights them, finds his sister, and comes home proud again.

Lewin's watercolors give us a genuine piece of New York City by offering portraits of each character and, indeed, each setting. The saloon with its derbied men and curving bar, the festoons of sausages against a white wall in the butcher shop, the crowded street lined with pushcarts, all are created for us to enter. The many nighttime scenes on the large, double-page spreads evoke an extra feeling of the time and place, produced by the limited lights of the gas lamps and candles. Grades 1-5.

Roslyn Bresnick-Perry, **Leaving for America**. Illustrated by Mira Reisberg. Children's Book Press, 1992. 32pp.

The author tells here of her experience leaving her extended family, favorite cousin, aunts, uncles, grandparents in a little Russian *shtetl* to come to America in 1929 when she was seven years old. The pain of saying goodbye to those she never saw again, of packing and being able to take so little, is recalled with humor. Some Yiddish is included. The fate of those relatives is left unsaid.

These memories are presented as mixed-media snapshots of the events in the text, which appears almost as extended captions on facing pages. Wide colored borders include pictures and symbols related to the paintings, for example, items packed in the big trunk, or Hebrew letters when the grandfather talks about reading the Holy Books. With one exception, a homage to Chagall's dream world of the *shtetl*, the style is child-like in simplifying the objects and in an awkward attempt at perspective. Clothing, hair styles, objects like the inevitable samovar, and even photographs, create a sense of history and place. K or Grades 1-4 or 5.

John Cech, **My Grandmother's Journey**. Illustrated by Sharon McGinley-Nally. Bradbury, 1991. 32pp.

This grandmother's tale of immigration to America begins back in Russia, when gypsies who cure her as a child predict great hardship. After she is married, she and her husband must endure the Russian Revolution, then World War II. They wander, helped by small miracles of friendship, survive German slave labor camps, and finally find safety in America. The text is long but matter-of-fact, filled with gritty details that make it real.

Visualized in a variety of layouts, using flatly applied mixed media, peasant-like patterns and decorations, even the human features, are stylized. In this story with a happy ending, grimmer events, like war and starvation, are pictured in a designed rather than realistic manner. Artifacts, uniforms, and buildings are represented literally enough to depict the story's Russian setting, while elaborate frames or borders soften the harsh realities. Endpapers show onion-domed churches and floating angels that suggest traditional painted icons. Grades 1-5.

Brett Harvey, **Immigrant Girl: Becky of Eldridge Street**. Illustrated by Deborah Kogan Ray. Holiday House, 1987. 40pp.

Becky herself tells her lengthy story, based on the real experiences of Jewish immigrants to the Lower East Side of New York City in 1910. Some of the grimmer aspects of life then are glossed over, but Becky does discuss the persecution the family feels. The work they all do, the crowded living conditions, the school on Rivington Street, shopping, summer heat and the ride to the park, all are described vividly, along with the preparations for the Sabbath and the Passover holiday. A glossary of the Yiddish words used is included.

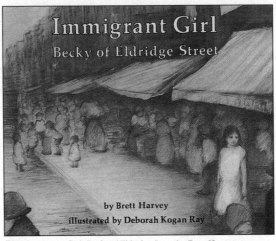

From *Immigrant Girl: Becky of Eldridge Street* by Brett Harvey. Illustrated by Deborah Kogan Ray. Copyright 1987. Reprinted with permission of Holiday House.

Black charcoal drawings are sensitively informative in visualizing the experiences told in the text. Naturalistic vignettes that can define the shapes of candlesticks but give more of an impression when depicting a crowd of strikers, street scenes under gaslight, the Saturday night bath in a washtub, the family Seder, all are filled with emotional impact as they add to this story that could be told about thousands of lives. Grades 1 or 2-5.

Ray has also illustrated Steven Kroll's *The Hokey-Pokey Man* (Holiday, 1989), a shorter, more simply told tale of the same area of New York in 1904. Two children have made friends with the man who sells ice cream from his cart, who hopes to make a lot of money from an invention of his cousin, a new idea that turns out to be the ice cream cone. Again Ray's drawings in sketchy black lines show real people of the time engaged in daily activities. Here she adds casually applied washy color, which brings vitality and a sense of gaiety to this happy story.

Riki Levinson, **Watch the Stars Come Out**. Illustrated by Diane Goode. Dutton, 1985. 32pp.

Here a grandmother tells her granddaughter the story her mother told her, of how she and her brother came on the big boat to America to join their parents. They arrive in New York harbor, and go through the immigration ordeal before their parents meet them. Finally the family is together again, so the girl can see the same stars that now shine in the sky for her great-granddaughter.

Color pencils model wonderfully detailed scenes framed in white and set on buff-colored pages. Crowds on the docks, on the deck, in the hold of the ship, on the streets, all are carefully articulated individual people. The scene on Hester Street in New York with its storefronts, pushcarts, and trolley is a real eye-grabber. These are real people in real settings, presented with the sort of warmth and sentiment expected from a grandmother telling an adoring child a family story. K or Grades 1-5.

Patricia Polacco, **The Keeping Quilt**. Simon & Schuster, 1988. 32pp.

This personal story begins with great-gramma Anna's arrival on the boat from Europe at Ellis Island. An outgrown dress inspires the making of a quilt with fabric from family members for the pieces to inspire memories. The quilt is the site of the proposal of Great-grandpa Sasha to Anna, and serves as the *chupa* for their wedding. It wraps their baby, is the canopy for her wedding, and so is part of the family history and memories until the present, when it has covered Patricia Polacco's daughter Traci.

Polacco's deft drawings here are touched with color for Anna's dress and babushka, and for the pieces of the quilt throughout the story. As always, the illustrations are full of details of time and place as well as with the actions, warmth and humanity of real people. K or Grades 1-4.

___, **Uncle Vova's Tree**. Philomel, 1989. 32pp.

Polacco reminisces about the traditional Russian Christmas celebration of her childhood on the farm in the American Midwest where her immigrant relatives have settled. The food is cooked, the tree decorated, paper stars taken for a sleigh ride, the outdoor tree decorated for the birds and animals, and finally the feast and presents enjoyed. That Christmas is the last with Uncle Vova, but the family remembers him afterward, as do the animals at the outdoor tree.

The artist continues to use her pencil to create faces and hands which define individual personalities. Paint adds details of dress and objects like the sled, holiday cakes, and the special tree. Two small, traditionally painted icons enhance the ties to the old country. Grades 1-4.

Background Books

Ellen Levine, **...If Your Name Was Changed at Ellis Island**. Illustrated by Wayne Parmenter. Scholastic, 1993. 80pp.

A clearly written compendium of answers to questions children may have about the experience of the more than 12 million people who came through Ellis Island after 1892. Parmenter's acrylic paintings picture specific events, some with fine detail. Grades 3 or 4-6.

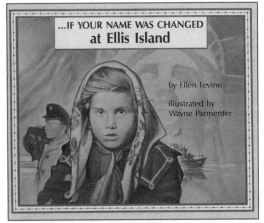

From ...*If Your Name Was Changed at Ellis Island* by Ellen Levine. Illustrated by Wayne Parmenter. Copyright 1993. Reprinted with permission of Scholastic.

William Kurelek, **They Sought a New World: The Story of European Immigration to North America**. Additional text by Margaret S. Englehart. Tundra hardback and paper, 1985. 48pp.

Kurelik's paintings are the basis for this picture of the immigrant experience of farm settlers. His mixed media, mostly full-page scenes pay attention to a multitude of details in a naturalistic style. With a focus on the human aspect, he depicts the village store, the family kitchen at Christmas, snow fun outside a one-room school, a railroad trestle over a gorge. Text fills in the facts, including the hardships, but emphasizing the universality of the experience. A map and population demographics are included. Grades 4-6 for text, younger for illustrations.

Notes

Section 9
Multicultural and Cross-Cultural Experiences

The books below represent the hopeful result of the work done with all the others: people of different cultures living, working, playing together, more conscious of their similarities than differences. We finally have reached a point where most picture books almost automatically include children of many colors in their illustrations. We expect this kind of recognition of our mixed cultures. But the books below try to go beyond this, to promote the message expressed by Anno in *All in a Day* below: "...the hope that by the time you grow up and learn more about such things, this earth will have become a better place for you to live on, a place where everyone is always happy and friendly." When so much of our news is of ethnic groups at war with each other, of continued examples of racial and religious persecution and prejudice, of expressed or implied hatred of one group by another, we feel the need to echo Rodney King's plea: "Can't we just get along?" In these books, we do.

Mitsumasa Anno, **All in a Day**. Philomel, 1986. 24pp.

Nine artists join Anno, as each takes a child from a different country through a day's activities on January 1. Eric Carle depicts Chicago; Raymond Briggs, Greenwich, England; Gian Calvi, Rio de Janeiro, Brazil; Leo and Diane Dillon, Nakuru, Kenya; Nicolai Ye. Popov, Moscow; Zhu Chengliang, Beijing, China; Akiko Hayashi, Tokyo, Japan; Ron Brooks, Sidney, Australia; and Anno himself, an "uninhabited" island. The "story" is simply told in few words and in the small but eloquent pictures by the distinguished illustrators. Each includes many pictorial references to the culture, but the connecting thread is the "communality of humankind." A note explains for parents and older readers the reasons for the time differences, as well as seasons and climate. K-Grade 4.

From *All in a Day* by Mitsumasa Anno. Copyright 1986. Reprinted with permission of Philomel.

Norah Dooley, **Everybody Cooks Rice**. Illustrated by Peter J. Thornton. Carolrhoda hardback, First Avenue Editions paper, 1991. 32pp.

Carrie's quest to round up her mooching brother for dinner takes her, in this wordy text, to the homes of families from Barbados, Puerto Rico, Vietnam, India, and Haiti. In each kitchen, native dishes with rice are being cooked and/or eaten, and Carrie samples them all. When she finally arrives back home, where her mother is cooking a rice dish from northern Italy, her brother is there, ready to eat more, but Carrie is full.

From *Everybody Cooks Rice* by Norah Dooley. Illustrated by Peter J. Thornton. Copyright 1991. Reprinted with permission of Carolrhoda.

The full-page illustrations show interiors and street scenes of an American suburb at dinner time. Although some of the people's appearance shows their origin, for example, the Hua's look Chinese, there are no other obvious signs of cultural differences. Pastels create rather detailed scenes of middle-class Americans going about routine tasks. Recipes for the dishes mentioned are an added plus. K or Grades 1-4.

Ina R. Friedman, **How My Parents Learned to Eat**. Illustrated by Allen Say. Houghton Mifflin hardback, 1984, paper, 1987. 32pp.

With a lengthy but easy-to-understand text, the author has written a first-person narrative told by a young girl whose father is American and mother Japanese. She explains how her parents met when her father, a sailor, was stationed in Yokahama, and her mother was a schoolgirl there. But her father never asked her mother out to dinner because he couldn't use chopsticks. The mother thought it was because she couldn't use a knife and fork. The father, who wanted to marry her before his ship was to leave, tried to learn to use chopsticks. Meanwhile she was trying to learn to use Western utensils. After much misunderstanding, they decide to marry and teach each other. Now, the narrator tells us, sometimes in their house they eat with knives and forks, and sometimes with chopsticks.

Say illustrates the story with rather literal scenes filled with the mundane details of modern Japan, including a few outdoor scenes with appropriate architecture, but focusing on interior settings that deal with eating. Utensils, food, seating arrangements in Japanese and Western restaurants are clearly depicted with black outlines and the palest of watercolor washes. Figures are naturally positioned in this spic-and-span world. There is even a suggestion of a textbook as the two cultures are put under a microscope. Grades 1-4.

Sarah Garland, **Billy and Belle**. Reinhardt/Viking, 1992. 28pp.

This simple story of a brother who takes his little sister to school while their father takes mother to the hospital never mentions that the family is in any way unusual. The kids go to school, sister lets everyone's pets loose and they have to be found, dad brings the kids home, later mother and new baby brother come back to join them.

The front endpapers show a sleeping couple in bed, while a young girl plays with a blond doll. The man is black and the woman is white; the girl is biracial. The pictures that follow make clear that these are mom, dad, and sister, that there's an older brother, and that mom is expecting a baby soon. Loose-jointed watercolors describe an English family's morning routine, then the special day at school for the preschooler in her brother's multiracial class. The back endpapers show the couple back asleep with the baby in a basket on the floor next to the bed. Lots of local detail creates a believable, sympathetic story. K-Grade 3.

Nigel Gray, **A Country Far Away**. Illustrated by Philippe Dupasquier. Orchard, 1988. 32pp.

In the simplest of sentences, a young boy tells what he does on ordinary days: at home, in school, with friends, shopping, celebrating the birth of a baby sister, enjoying a cousin's visit.

The mid-page caption-like sentences separate two sequences of pictures: the top describes rural African life and the bottom a suburban Western life. Each double page is divided into two or more pictures all directed to the event in the boy's life in each place, showing each playing soccer or going swimming. Transparent watercolors over black line drawings ably make comparisons between the weather,

From *A Country Far Away* by Nigel Gray. Illustrated by Philippe Dupasquier. Copyright 1988. Reprinted with permission of Orchard.

landscape, costume, buildings, and general atmosphere around the brown-skinned Africans and the primarily pink-skinned Westerners who are never mentioned in the text. Both life styles are portrayed positively, in great detail, with a concluding page showing each boy holding a world map as he expresses the desire to travel and "make a friend" there. This book has been criticized because the area in Africa is generalized from several, and because of the depiction of the Africans themselves. Does this dilute the purpose? K-Grade 3.

Daisaku Ikeda, **Over the Deep Blue Sea**. Illustrated by Brian Wildsmith. English version by Geraldine McCaughrean. Random House, 1993. 28pp.

When their parents' work moves the family to a strange new island, Akiko and her brother Hiroshi feel strange and lonely, until Pablo shows them all the wonders of his island, including nesting sea turtles. One day Pablo won't play with them any more. His grandmother has told him how people from Akiko and Hiroshi's country once attacked Pablo's island. Angry Hiroshi sets out in a canoe in a storm. Pablo picks him out of the water, but both are almost lost in the sea before a ship picks them up. The ship captain tells them how ocean currents have always carried people from place to place, making all from the same sea really brothers. Friendship surfaces again, as the sea turtles symbolically hatch and begin their voyage back to the sea.

Also symbolically the front endpapers show a churning sea with frothy whitecaps while the back endpapers illustrate a serenely calm sea. In between, Wildsmith visualizes a Pacific Island's beauty on large double pages, exploiting his usual mixed-media complex style. The vegetation is technicolored, the mountain range purple-blue, and a sunset glows with red radiance. The wrecked battleship left from the invasion is starkly, grimly gray in the deep blue waters. The children and boats are small pieces of the larger scenes, with no close-ups. Nature is pictured as the force that makes them friends. Grades 1-4.

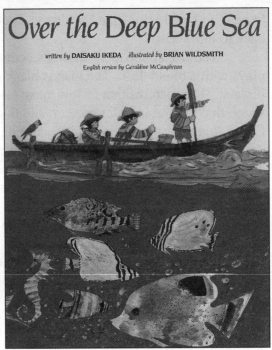

From *Over the Deep Blue Sea* by Daisaku Ikeda. Illustrated by Brian Wildsmith. Copyright 1993. Reprinted with permission of Random House.

Klaus Kordon, **The Big Fish**. Illustrated by The Tjong Khing. Macmillan, 1992. 28pp.

The multicolored folks in their costumes from around the world happily holding hands and dancing across the bottom of the endpapers introduce this quiet plea for tolerance. In a variation on the fairy tale, a fisherman and his wife help a fish stranded after a storm. He offers to grant them a wish. They have always wanted a child. When they climb on his back, he takes them magically through the sea, first to huts by a shore, where a small girl sits alone. She could be their daughter, the fish tells them. But they reject her angrily because she is black. Next he takes them to a small boy fishing near houses on stilts. But he is brown, so also denied. When they scorn "yellow" children as well, the angry fish leaves them to drown. The people save their lives, but reject them because they are "white." They build a home with the children and decide to stay.

The couple's lively adventures are given a lively interpretation in pictures using a nervous black outline and thin watercolor washes. There are enough details of greenery, buildings, and artifacts to create specific places without clutter. The larger underwater scenes present a wide variety of sea life quite naturalistically. People are made convincing in gesture and action with minimal anatomical details. A delightful touch is the pseudo-Oriental painting of the landscape where the "yellow" children live. Grades 1 or 2-6.

Pili Mandelbaum, **You Be Me: I'll Be You**. Kane/Miller, 1989. 36pp.

In the simplest of terms, the Belgian author deals with profound questions. Anna's father is "white," Anna is "brown," and convinced that she's not pretty. She wants to look like her father. Anna decides her mother is like the coffee they make, her father like the milk, and she's the coffee-milk or cafe-au-lait. She prefers her father's hair as well. If you can accept the fact that they go out to meet mother with father's hair in pigtails, his face covered with coffee grounds, and Anna's with powder, then this silliness, which embarrasses mother, can lead to a provocative discussion. The author also has them comment on how everybody seems to be curling their straight hair or uncurling the curly, or tanning their skin when it's white; nobody seems happy with their skin or hair.

Collage using fabrics and papers against faintly spatter-painted backgrounds create believable characters and everyday objects. Full-page pictures comfortably include the few lines of caption-like text. The artist is able to show the actions of a loving father and energetic young daughter convincingly. Grades 1-3.

Angela Shelf Medearis, **Dancing with the Indians**. Illustrated by Samuel Byrd. Holiday House, 1991. 32pp.

Inspired by the experiences of her ancestors, the author's simple verses tell of a young girl's visit in the 1930s to an Indian powwow. The Seminoles, forced to move to Oklahoma, accepted the author's great-grandfather, an escaped slave, as a member of their tribe. The family has included African Americans and Native Americans ever since. The text simply

From *Dancing with the Indians* by Angela Shelf Medearis. Illustrated by Samuel Byrd. Copyright 1991. Reprinted with permission of Holiday House.

celebrates the rhythm and feeling of the dance along with the memories it provokes. The story has been criticized for some supposedly patronizing comments about Native Americans, rather than appreciated for its message of togetherness.

Full-page watercolor paintings show environment and dress of the Seminoles, but the emphasis is on the atmosphere of the Ribbon, Rattlesnake, and Stomp dances that eventually involve the young narrator and her brother. Campfires produce melodramatic shadows and movements in illustrations that evoke moods more than they specify. The final double-page painting of a vast brown landscape with a yellow dawn breaking makes a proper restful contrast to the more frenetic scenes of the dancing. K-Grade 3.

Patricia Polacco, **Chicken Sunday**. Philomel, 1992. 32pp.

___, **Mrs. Katz and Tush**. Bantam Little Rooster, 1992. 32pp.

In *Chicken Sunday* Polacco tells a story from her childhood, when Stewart and Winston were her "brothers," and their gramma Eula Mae Walker became hers as well. The children are saving money to buy Miss Eula a hat she admires in Mr. Kodinski's shop. They get to know the old shopkeeper, who helps them earn money by selling the *pysanky* Easter eggs that Polacco's mother helps them make. Miss Eula proudly wears the hat to church on Easter Sunday. She lives on in memory, and the brothers remain friends of the author today. The loving African-American family, their acceptance of the "white" narrator, Mr. Kodinski's prickly behavior after eggs are tossed at his shop, perhaps because of his Russian-Jewish background, all this is woven into a lengthy narrative full of loving acceptance of differences.

Larnel's mother checks regularly on Mrs. Katz, the sad and lonely Jewish widow of *Mrs. Katz and Tush*. One day the young African American brings the widow a kitten to keep her company; she names it Tush. Keeping his promise to help care for Tush, Larnel gets to know Mrs. Katz better as she tells him about her life, pointing out how both her people and his have known persecution. Tush is lost and found, then has kittens. Mrs. Katz prepares a Passover Seder for herself and Larnel. She gradually becomes part of his family, sharing the joys and sorrows. Since she has no children, it is Larnel who says the traditional prayers for her after she dies.

Both books are illustrated in a similar style, full of portraits done in pencil and paint, with added specific objects for the ethnic settings, from photos of Miss Eula's family and decorated eggs to church choir robes and menorah. All are filled with the strong emotional content of Polacco's love. Grades 1-5 or 6.

Chris Raschka, **Yo! Yes?** Orchard, 1993. 32pp.

From *Yo! Yes?* by Chris Raschka. Copyright 1993. Reprinted with permission of Orchard.

Raschka's "story" is so much more than its one monosyllabic word per page. Two male characters from different cultures meet. One is dark-complexioned and "hip," confrontational down to the loose laces on his sneakers. The other is lighter-skinned, trousered and jacketed, wary.

Equally "monosyllabic" pictures created with charcoal and watercolors depict the boys' reactions. Each appears on facing pages with tinted backgrounds and the word painted boldly in black above them. Their gestures and actions tend to be exaggerated. They convey their meanings in the manner of caricature while maintaining their personalities and fundamental humanity. The final page, showing them holding hands and leaping up off the top edge of the page together, is pure joy. Grades 1-6.

Michael J. Rosen, **Elijah's Angel: A Story for Chanukah and Christmas**. Illustrated by Aminah Brenda Lynn Robinson. Harcourt Brace, 1992. 32pp.

Both author and illustrator knew the barber and self-taught woodcarver Elijah Pierce, and have tried to make the story true to his character and spirit. Nine-year-old Michael, a regular visitor to Elijah's barbershop, tells how he got the angel of the title the year that Christmas Eve and the first night of Chanukah coincided. Elijah and his work are concerned with Jesus and the Bible, while Michael is Jewish. When Elijah gives him a Christmas guardian angel, a "graven image" not allowed in Jewish homes, Michael is afraid his parents will be upset. But they assure him it is an angel of friendship. Michael gives Elijah a menorah in exchange, which Elijah lights in the barbershop window each night for Chanukah. Information on Elijah Pierce is included.

In keeping with Pierce's use of house paints on his carvings, Robinson here uses them on cloth in many textless double-page scenes as well as for a variety of vignettes in the lengthy text. Black outlines blend with the opaque intensities of these paints to produce detail-crammed scenes of the barbershop and the neighborhood as well as several of the carvings. Expressionistic in their exaggeration of forms, like those of Pierce's hands which express the strength of a life devoted to cutting hair and carving wood, the illustrations are full of good feelings among people. K-Grade 4.

John Rowe, **Jack the Dog**. Picture Book Studio, 1993. 32pp.

This zany dog adventure that turns out to be a dream begins when Jack gets lost in a London fog and wakes up on a ship bound for Japan. Arriving in winter snow and naturally wanting a cup of tea, Jack is told by a crow that he must take a bath and wear a kimono now that he's in Japan. After his bath, two dogs assure him that he must have a wig to wear with the kimono. A cat insists he must also carry a fan, and an old monkey adds a paper umbrella to his list, while directing him to the Kabuki theater alley. Finally properly attired, Jack is called from his green tea to wake up and have his usual tea at home.

Rowe perceives the visual world in ways that eliminate all but the most essential details. Scumbled colors provide backgrounds for the animal actors, each portrayed with distinctive character. They wear clothes with tongue-in-cheek patterns: the monkey's jacket has bananas, a dog's coat has bones. Each acrylic painting is set with wide white borders that match the size of facing gray rectangles housing a white text, making for visual elegance. The logic of these dreamy surrealities points at some universal cultural communalities. Be it green or brown, a fellow needs his tea. Grades 1-5.

Anne Shelby, **Potluck**. Illustrated by Irene Trivas. Orchard, 1991. 32pp.

Alpha and Betty's jolly potluck meal is really an alphabet of foods. Children with names beginning with A to Z in all shapes, sizes, and colors arrive, each with a food which may or may not reflect their cultural heritage.

Focus is on the foods, especially the double-page extravaganza of the front of Garbanzo's Bakery overflowing with breads and cakes, or on Lonnie's huge truckful of lasagna. Opaque gouache paints create a string of huggable youngsters showing off their favorite foods with brushstrokes of background color. K-Grade 3.

Marilyn Singer, **Nine O'clock Lullaby**. Illustrated by Frane Lessac. HarperCollins, 1991. 32pp.

Beginning with 9:00 p.m. in Brooklyn, New York, we go around the globe, seeing what is happening at 10:00 p.m. in Puerto Rico, 2:00 a.m. in England, 3:00 a.m. in Zaire and Switzerland, through Moscow, Guangzhou, Japan, Sidney, Samoa, Los Angeles, Mexico, Wisconsin, and back to Brooklyn. A sentence or phrase is all that is said about some locations, poetic evocations describe more about others. An explanation of how time zones work is included.

Lessac's child-like paintings are the unifying factor in these scenes of life from different countries. Double pages show people engaged in typical activities: Indian women in saris drawing water from a village well, an Australian extended family having a picnic in a Sidney park, Inuits playing the toss-up game, a Chinese town's population on bicycles. Several local animals and objects help specify the culture. But the overall sense of common human values and the oneness of the earth blur the differences. K-Grades 3 or 4.

Irene Trivas, **Annie...Anya: A Month in Moscow**. Orchard, 1992. 32pp.

At first Annie doesn't like Moscow much. Except for the subway and the circus, she finds it all too strange: food, language, even different ABCs. When her mother and father must begin their month's work as doctors, Annie meets her namesake Anya at the day-care center. She begins to learn Russian as she makes other friends with Anya's help. She visits Anya's home, her ballet class, and finds it hard to say *Dosvidaye* when it's time to go home to America.

From *Potluck* by Anne Shelby. Illustrated by Irene Trivas. Copyright 1991. Reprinted with permission of Orchard.

From *Annie...Anya* by Irene Trivas. Copyright 1992. Reprinted with permission of Orchard.

Black-ink lines create the myriad details of a modern Russian setting, while transparent watercolors add body and mood. Scenes of Moscow include the waiting lines outside stores in drab buildings, the "roller coaster" escalators in the subway, and the crowds in Red Square. The loose drawing creates believable people. Annie's personality is particularly developed as she emerges from her negative shell to be an enthusiastic participant in Russian life. Informative and upbeat are the jolly picture on the jacket of the two girls in front of St. Basil's and the final one of them hugging goodbye. K-Grade 3.

Background Books

Carol Gelber, **Masks Tell Stories**. Millbrook Press, 1993. 72pp.

In describing masks used for celebrations, theater, and other occasions around the world, this text discusses many cultures. Illustrations are color and black-and-white photographs, some not clear. Grades 3 or 4-6.

Margery Burns Knight, **Talking Walls**. Illustrated by Anne Sibley O'Brien. Tilbury House, 1992. 40pp.

This introduction to 14 walls around the world uses a large double-page spread for illustrating each wall plus text concerning its political, religious, or esthetic significance. Additional information is at the end of the book. Pastels are used for adequate representations impressionistically depicting the wall with humans to show the scale. The walls range from the Great Wall of China to the Berlin Wall. Grades 2 or 3-6.

Maxine B. Rosenberg, **Living in Two Worlds**. Lothrop, 1986. 46pp.

Children of biracial families talk about their lives and how they feel about the challenges they face. George Ancona's clear black-and-white photographs show families together, in celebrations, and children in other places like school or with grandparents. This is multiculturalism in action. Grades 2 or 3-6.

Jane Yolen, editor, **Street Rhymes Around the World**. Wordsong/Boyds Mills, 1992. 40pp.

Counting rhymes, finger-play jingles, jump-rope refrains, all sorts of children's fun from countries everywhere are included, some bilingual. Seventeen illustrators have each done pictures for the different countries, some more well-crafted, and some more culturally relevant than others. Just let children enjoy this fun from many lands. K-Grade 4.

<u>Notes</u>

Appendix A
Additional Resources: Nonfiction Series

Quality varies among the titles in any series, but all of the series listed here include useful information. They have been published in the last few years. Encyclopedias are useful as well.

The Ancient World. Silver Burdett. 48pp. Grades 4-6, younger for pictures.

Brief remarks on all aspects of life and culture, religion, government, art and architecture, transportation and communication. Include maps, glossary. Cultures include Aztecs, Chinese, Egyptians, First Africans, Incas, Japanese, and Mayas.

Children of the World. Gareth Stevens. 64pp. Grades 3-6, younger for pictures.

Chronicles daily life of children. Reference information on history, culture, religion, and language. Maps and glossary. Seems to aim to include all countries.

Count your way through... Carolrhoda. 24pp. Grades 2 or 3-6.

Includes numbers 1-10, pronunciation, facts about the country that relate in some way to each number, undistinguished illustrations. Countries covered include Africa, Arab world, China, India, Japan, Korea, Mexico, Russia, etc.

Enchantment of the World. Children's Press. 121-128pp. Grade 5 and up.

Includes geography, history, religion, culture, government today, and brief fact summary. Photographs are small but clear and informative. The length of the books does not vary despite the size and complexity of the countries covered. Quality not consistent.

Families Around the World. Watts. 32pp. Grades 4-6.

Shows life of a family in the countries covered. Note there is no aboriginal family in the volume on Australia. Similar to the Lerner series below.

Families the World Over. Lerner. 32pp. Grades 4-6.

Good summary of family life. Has an aboriginal family as well as other families in Australia. Many countries included.

Inside... Franklin Watts. 32pp. Grades K or 1-3.

Oversize volumes, similar to Take a Trip below. Netherlands, France, and Germany among countries included.

New True. Lerner. 48pp. Grades 2-6.

Covers land, people, history, crafts, and life today. New terms are defined. Color photographs. Some groups included are the Apache, Maya, Zimbabwe, Asia, Australia.

Original Peoples. Rourke. 48pp. Grades 3-6.

Covers where these groups came from, how they live, food, clothing, shelter, occupations, life today. Color photographs and maps. Includes Bedouin, Eskimos, Maoris, Aborigines of Australia, Plains Indians, South Pacific Islanders, Indians of the Andes, Indians of the Amazon, Bushmen of Central Africa, Zulus of Southern Africa.

Religions of the World. Watts. 45pp. Grades 4-6.

Includes basic information. Photographs. Buddhism and Hinduism are among the titles.

Take a Trip. Watts. 32pp. K or Grades 1-3.

Covers the usual areas of life so a child can understand. Large print, good size color photographs. Many are out of date, however.

The World Heritage. Children's Press (UNESCO affiliated) 32pp. Grades 3-6, younger for pictures.

The Land of the Pharaohs, *The Chinese Empire*, and *The Mayan Civilization* are currently available.

The World's Children. Lerner/Carolrhoda. 48pp. Grades 3-6.

Includes brief information on geography and history. Color photographs. *Children of China*, *Children of India*, *Children of Nepal* are among the titles available.

Appendix B

Sources of Arts and Crafts From Many Cultures

Catalogs from the museums and organizations below offer books, reproductions of artifacts and other items from many cultures.

The American Museum of Natural History
Central Park West at 79th St.
New York, New York 10024-5192

The Art Institute of Chicago Museum Shop
Michigan Avenue at Adams Street
Chicago, Illinois 60603

Care Package Catalog
P.O. Box 684
Holmes, Pennsylvania 19043

Criznac
P.O. Box 65928
Tucson, Arizona 85728-5928

The Hemmeter Collection
711 East Gardens Blvd.
Gardena, California 90248

Museum Collections
306 Dartmouth St.
Boston, Massachusetts 02116

Oxfam America
P. O. Box 821
Lewiston, Maine 04240

The Smithsonian Institution
Department 0006
Washington, D.C. 20073-0006

Southwest Indian Foundation
P.O.Box 86
Gallup, New Mexico 87302-0001

UNICEF
1 Children's Boulevard
P.O. Box 182233
Chattanooga, Tennessee 37422

Appendix C
Publishers with Lists of Multicultural Materials Available

African Books Collective Ltd.
The Jam Factory
27 Park End At.
Oxford OX1 1HU England
Ask for: Books for Multicultural
Education

Albert Whitman & Co.
6340 Oakton Street
Morton Grove, Illinois 60053-2723
Ask for: Books that Celebrate Cultural
Diversity

Bantam Doubleday Dell Publishing
Group
666 Fifth Avenue
New York, New York 10103
Ask for: Cultural Diversity

Black Butterfly Children's Books
P.O. Box 461
Village Station
New York, New York 10014
Ask for: Catalog

Brodart Books Division
500 Arch Street
Williamsport, Pennsylvania 17705
Ask for: Exploring Cultural Diversity

Carolrhoda Books
241 First Avenue North
Minneapolis, Minnesota 55401
Ask for: Multicultural Books

Cattermole 20th Century Children's
Books
9880 Fairmount Rd.
Newbury, Ohio 44065
Ask for: Catalog 17, Japanese Picture
Books

Children's Book Press
1461 Ninth Ave.
San Francisco, California 94112
Ask for: Catalog

China Books and Periodicals, Inc.
2929 Twenty-fourth St.
San Francisco, California 94110
Ask for: Catalog

Clarion Books
215 Park Ave. South
New York, New York 10003
Ask for: Multicultural Books from
Clarion

Farrar, Straus & Giroux
19 Union Square West
New York, New York 10003
Ask for: A Multicultural Listing

Greenfield Review Press
2 Middle Grove Road
P.O. Box 308
Greenfield Center, New York 12833
Ask for: Native American Authors
Distribution Project

HarperCollins Children's Books
10 East 53rd Street
New York, New York 10022
Ask for: Widening Horizons

The Highsmith Company
W5527 Highway 106
P.O. Box 800
Fort Atkinson, Wisconsin 53538-0800
Ask for: Multicultural Publishers
Exchange

Intercultural Press
P.O. Box 700
Yarmouth, Maine 04096
Ask for: Catalog

Just Us Books
301 Main Steet
Suite 22-24
Orange, New Jersey 07050
Ask for: Catalog

Kane/Miller Book Publishers
P.O. Box 8515
La Jolla, California 92038-8515
Ask for: Catalog

Lee & Low Books
228 East 45th Street
New York, New York 10017
Ask for: Catalog

Lerner Publications Company
241 First Ave. North
Minneapolis, Minnesota 55401
Ask for: Multicultural Books

Little, Brown & Co.
34 Beacon St.
Boston, Massachusetts 02108
Ask for: Little, Brown Multicultural
Library

Macmillan Children's Group
866 Third Avenue
New York, New York 10022
Ask for: Multicultural titles

William Morrow & Co.
1350 Avenue of the Americas
New York, New York 10019
Ask for: Multicultural Books list

Native Books
P.O. Box 37095
Honolulu, Hawaii 96837
Ask for: News

Orchard Books
5450 North Cumberland Avenue
Chicago, Illinois 60656-1484
Ask for: Multicultural Collection

Penguin USA
375 Hudson Street
New York, New York 10014
Ask for: Books of Multicultural Interest,
Puffin Books Thematic Collections

Putnam & Grosset Group
200 Madison Avenue
New York, New York 10016
Ask for: The Multicultural World of
Putnam & Grosset and Celebrating our
Ethnic Diversity

Random House
Public Relations & Library Marketing
225 Park Avenue South
New York, New York 10003
Ask for: Explore Cultural Diversity

Rizzoli International Publications
300 Park Avenue South
New York, New York 10010-5399
Ask for: Multicultural Books for All
Ages

Scholastic Inc.
730 Broadway
New York, New York 10003
Ask for: Multicultural Titles and A
World of Many Cultures

Simon & Schuster Children's Books
15 Columbus Circle
New York, New York 10023
Ask for: Multicultural Titles

Franklin Watts
5450 North Cumberland Avenue
Chicago, Illinois 60656-1484
Ask for: Multicultural Collection

Appendix D
Bibliography

Judy Allen, Earlene McNeill, and Velma Ashmidt, *Cultural Awareness for Children*. Addison-Wesley, 1992. 254pp.

"Art as Culture," *School Arts*, April 1993 issue.

James A. Banks and Sherry A McGee Banks, *Multicultural Education: Issues and Perspectives*. Allyn and Bacon, 1989. 337pp.

Robert C. Branch and Michelle R. Rice, "Cultural Sensitivity in Media Selection," *Ohio Media Spectrum*, Spring 1992, pp. 25-29.

Carolyn S. Brodie, "Keys to Multicultural Resources," *School Library Media Activities Monthly*, April 1992, pp. 42-43.

Canada's Aboriginal Peoples. Special issue of *Canada Today/d'aujourdhui*, Vol. 23, No. 1, 1993. Canadian Embassy. 15pp.

"Curriculum Guidelines for Multicultural Education" Prepared by the NCSS Task Force on Ethnic Studies Curriculum Guidelines, *Social Education*, September 1992, pp. 274-294.

Barbara Elleman, "From Many Shores," *Book Links*, July 1993, pp. 11-15.

EMIE Bulletin, issued quarterly by the Ethnic Materials and Information Exchange Round Table of the American Library Association.

Encyclopedia of Educational Research, 6th edition, Vol. 3. Macmillan, 1992.

Violet Harris, "Multicultural Curriculum: African American Children's Literature," *Young Children* Vol. 46, No. 2, January 1991, pp. 37-44.

Betsy Hearne, "Cite the Source: Reducing Cultural Chaos in Picture Books, Part One" *School Library Journal*, July 1993, pp. 23-27.

Journal of Multicultural and Cross-cultural Research in Art Education, published yearly by United States Society for Education through Art.

Milton Kleg, "On the NCSS Curriculum Guidelines for Multicultural Education" *Social Education*, February 1993, pp. 58-59.

Ginny Moore Kruse, "No Single Season: Multicultural Literature for All Children," *Wilson Library Bulletin*, February 1992, pp. 30-37.

Ginny Moore Kruse and Kathleen T. Horning, *Multicultural Literature for Children and Young Adults: A Selected Listing of Books 1980-1990 By and About People of Color*, 3rd edition. University of Wisconsin-Madison Cooperative Children's Book Center, 1991. 78pp.

Susan Kuklin, *Speaking Out: Teenagers Take on Race, Sex, and Identity*. Putnam, 1993. 165pp.

Marjorie H. and Peter Li, *Understanding Asian Americans: A Curriculum Resource Guide*. Neal-Schuman, 1990. 186pp.

Suzanne Lo and Ginny Lee, "What Stories Do We Tell Our Children?" *Emergency Librarian*, May-June 1993, pp. 14-18.

Roberta Long and Fran D. Perkins, *Celebrating African American Literature: A Selected Bibliography of Children's Books by African American Authors*. University of Alabama at Birmingham, 1991. 17pp.

James Lynch, *Education for Citizenship in a Multicultural Society*. Cassell, 1992. 122pp.

James Lynch, *Multicultural Education in a Global Society*. Falmer, 1989. 191pp.

James Lynch, *Multicultural Education: Principles and Practice*. Routledge and Kegan Paul, 1986. 230pp.

Donnarae MacCann and Olga Richard, "Picture Books and Native Americans: An Interview with Naomi Caldwell-Wood," *Wilson Library Bulletin*, February 1993, pp. 30-34, 112.

Sharron L. McElmeel, *Bookpeople: A Multicultural Album*. Libraries Unlimited, 1992. 170pp.

Lyn Miller-Lachman, "The Audience for Multicultural Literature," *Journal Of Youth Services in Libraries*, Winter, 1993, pp. 163-165.

Lyn Miller-Lachman, *Our Family, Our Friends, Our World: An Annotated Guide to Significant Multicultural Books for Children and Teenagers*. Bowker, 1992. 710pp.

The Multicolored Mirror: Cultural Substance in Literature for Children and Young Adults. Edited by Merri V. Lindgren for the Cooperative Children's Book Center. Highsmith Press, 1991. 195pp.

Multicultural Review. Published quarterly by Greenwood Publishing Group, Inc.

The Multicultural Teaching Resource Guide. The Ohio State University Center for Teaching Excellence, 1992. 34pp.

"Museum Showcase: Museums Offer Classrooms the Treasures of Many Cultures," *Teaching Tolerance*, Fall 1992, pp. 16-19.

Rosalind Ragans and Jane Rhoades, *Understanding Art.* Glencoe/Macmillan/McGraw-Hill, 1992, 334pp.

Patricia G. Ramsey, Edwina Battle Vold, and Leslie R. Williams, *Multicultural Education: A Source Book.* Garland, 1989.

Timothy V. Rasinski and Nancy D. Padak, "Multicultural Learning through Children's Literature," *Language Arts*, October 1990, pp. 576-580.

Diane Ravitch, "Multiculturalism: E Pluribus Plures," *The Key Reporter*, Autumn 1990, pp. 1-4.

Hazel Rochman, *Against Borders: Promoting Books for a Multicultural World.* American Library Association, 1993. 288pp.

Arthur M. Schlesinger, Jr., *The Disuniting of America: Reflections on a Multicultural Society.* Norton, 1992. 160pp.

Jo Miles Schuman, *Art from Many Hands: Multicultural Art Projects for Home and School.* Davis, 1984. 256pp.

Christine E. Sleeter and Carl A. Grant, "An Analysis of Multicultural Education in the United States" in *The Harvard Education Review*, November 1987, pp. 421-444.

Teaching Tolerance, published semi-annually by the Southern Poverty Law Center.

Through Indian Eyes: The Native Experience in Books for Children. Edited by Beverly Slapin and Doris Seale. New Society Publishers, 1992.

Venture into Cultures: A Resource Book of Multicultural Materials and Programs. Edited by Carla D. Hayden. American Library Association, 1992. 165pp.

Phoebe Yeh, "Multicultural Publishing: The Best and Worst of Times," *Journal of Youth Services in Libraries*, Winter 1993, pp. 157-160.

Enid Zimmerman and Gilbert Clark, "Resources for Teaching Art From a Multicultural Point of View," *ERIC: ART Bulletin*, September 1992.

Picture Book Index

Make this your best year ever!
Put Library Talk or The Book Report
at the top of your stack.

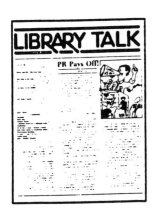

"Just received my first issue of LIBRARY TALK and read it from cover to cover. It's exactly the magazine I've been looking for."
....Portland, OR

LIBRARY TALK--the magazine librarians love--is filled with information that's vitally important, engagingly written, superbly organized.

FEATURE ARTICLES--written by elementary school librarians for elementary school librarians.

FILED ABOVE THE ROD--straight talk about the challenges as well as the joys of being an elementary librarian.

SHOPTALK--dozens of ideas to make you cry "Eureka!"

LIBRARY ASSISTANTS--a column devoted to the unique and diverse concerns of paraprofessionals and part-time workers.

BOOKBAG--news from publishers, info on free or inexpensive materials, the scoop on general interest books.

HOLIDAY BOOKS--annual roundup of new holiday books for children.

REVIEW COLUMNS--experienced librarians evaluate these books for you: Easy Readers, Fiction for Grades 3-4, Fiction for Grades 5 & Up, Nonfiction, Mysteries and Fantasies, Books in Spanish, Traditional Stories, Reference Series, Audiovisuals, and Software.

"THE BOOK REPORT is the one magazine I make time to read cover to cover."
....Leetonia, OH

THE BOOK REPORT--the magazine librarians respect--is filled with right-on reviews, inside info on authors, and tons of tips to make your school year sizzle.

THEME SECTIONS--features articles by school librarians on a different theme in each issue.

TIPS & OTHER BRIGHT IDEAS--an all-around favorite. Brief how-to's, innovative ideas and solutions to puzzling problems.

REVIEWS--written by more than 160 experienced librarians who describe, evaluate and make purchase recommendations about new books in a variety of categories.

BOOKS & OTHER THINGS--news about library products, free and inexpensive materials, and special interest books.

THE COMPUTING LIBRARIAN--the low-down on library computer applications.

AUTHOR PROFILES--interviews and background info on authors who write for teens.

PAPERBACK RACK--learn the facts about expanding your collection with recent trade paperbacks that duplicate popular hardback titles.

BACKTALK--a forum for your peeves, praise, quizzes, essays, and humor.

Our Professional Growth Series Keys in on Your Needs!

The notebooks, workbooks, and special reports of the Professional Growth Series are your keys to ideas that are working in school libraries across the country. All of these publications have been developed by school library media specialists who want to share what works best in their schools.

Announcing! **Multicultural Picture Books: Art for Understanding Others** by Kenneth & Sylvia Marantz. Outstanding multicultural picture books are identified and critiqued for quality of their illustrations, their reflection of the art of the culture, and their sensitivity to the spirit of the characters involved. The book includes an annotated bibliography and sources of information. Softcover. 200+ pages. ISBN 0-938865-22-6. $28.95. Available December 1993.

PGS Notebooks

The following publications are offered in 3-ring binders with colorful tabbed dividers. This format allows for easy information retrieval and quick reference. And, you can easily add your own materials!

Announcing! **Skills for Life: Library Information Literacy for Grades K-6**.
This notebook is filled with sample lessons, all written and tested by practicing professionals. Sections are: Skills Cross-Reference; Sample Skills Curriculum; Orientation and Use of the Library; Appreciation and Forms of Fiction Literature; Information Books—Non-Fiction; Understanding and Using the Card Catalog—Card or Automated; Research and Study Skills; Bibliography; and Index. 3-ring binder. 300+ pages. ISBN 0-938865-19-6. $34.95. Available October 1993.

Announcing! **Skills for Life: Library Information Literacy for Grades 6-8**.
This notebook is filled with sample lesson plans written by and tested by practicing professionals. Sections are: Information Skills for the 21st Century; Getting Ready for Research at the Secondary Level; Reading Motivation; and Evaluation. 3-ring binder. 200+ pages. ISBN 0-938865-20-X. $34.95. Available November 1993.

Announcing! **Skills for Life: Library Information Literacy for Grades 9-12**.
This skills notebook is filled with sample lesson plans written by and tested by practicing professionals. Sections are: Rethinking Theory; The New Technology of Learning; CD-ROM; Online Database Searching; Local Area Network; Electronic Bulletin Boards; Laser Discs; Multimedia; Robotics; Special Curricular Challenges—ESL, Vocational Education, and Library Skills for Credit; Learning Partnerships; The Future; and Bibliography. 3-ring binder. 200+ pages. ISBN 0-938865-21-8. $34.95. Available October 1993.

Announcing! **Looking Great with Video** by Augie E. Beasley. This practical self-help book covers what can be done with limited funds and a lot of imagination! Sections are: Introduction; Language of Video; Script Writing; Audio Fundamentals; Lighting Fundamentals; Editing Fundamentals; Special Effects; Graphics; and Projects. 3-ring binder. 200+ pages. ISBN 0-938865-23-4. $34.95. Available November 1993.

Announcing! **Winning Friends for the School Library** by Valerie Childress. Childress, awarded the John Cotton Dana Special Award for Public Relations in 1991 and 1992, has packaged her secret to success in a handbook of PR ideas, projects, programs and techniques for the school library. Sections are: Working with Students, Principals, Teachers, Staff Members, and Parents; Making the Library Inviting; Making and Keeping the School Library Visible; Projects and Contests; Spreading the Word with Media; Follow Up Tactics; and Writing and Publishing Your Own Professional Articles. 3-ring binder. 125+ pages. ISBN 0-938865-24-2. $28.95. Available October 1993.

New! **Instant Art Notebook**. The notebook contains all five instant art packages published from 1987 to 1992, but divided into these major categories: Curriculum; Reading Motivation; Newsletters, Memos, and Announcements; Holidays; and Special Events & Awards. Sections include ideas for use. 3-ring binder. 140 pages. ISBN 0-938865-17-X. $34.95. October 1992.

Announcing! **Instant Art VI**. Add to your Instant Art Notebook with this year's new package. 25 sheets of fresh illustrations for the school year. ISBN 0-938865-28-5. $10.95. Available September 1993.

The Elementary School Librarian's Desk Reference: Library Skills & Management by Alice H. Yucht. Finally, a professional resource for the elementary school library. This practical handbook can be used by supervisors, building-level librarians, and paraprofessionals as a source of adaptable ideas and guidance. Covered are: Roles & Responsibilities; Evaluation; Daily Management; Selection & Circulation; Weeding & Inventory; Aides & Volunteers; Computers; Teaching Library Skills; Public Relations; and Professional Resources. 3-ring binder. 371 pages. ISBN 0-938865-05-6. $38.95. April 1992.

Making It With Media by Augie E. Beasley. This step-by-step guide shows you how to be a multimedia librarian! Included are directions ranging from such high-tech endeavors as creating exciting computer graphics and producing professional-looking videotapes to using lettering techniques to enliven old stand-bys such as bulletin board displays. You'll also learn about photography, transparency design, and teaching AV production. 3-ring binder. 246 pages. ISBN 0-938865-07-2. $34.95. April 1992.

Lessons for the Library Student Staff by Toni Pray. This informative manual is organized in a lesson format to help instruct student staff in a meaningful and efficient way. Lessons include Staff Policies; A Staff Welcome; Shelving; Circulation Procedures; Indexes, Periodicals & Alphabetizing; The Periodical Room; Office Tour; Dry Mounting & Laminating; Teaching & Assisting Other Students; Special Duties; Discipline Policies; and Staff Grading Policies. Each lesson includes instruction sheets, review sheets, worksheets, and quizzes. 3-ring binder. 234 pages. ISBN 0-938865-11-0. $29.95. March 1992.

THE BOOK REPORT & LIBRARY TALK Author Profile Collection. A collection of 21 author and artist profiles that have appeared in THE BOOK REPORT and LIBRARY TALK. Includes Avi; Arnold Adoff; Marion Dane Bauer; Carole Byard; Orson Scott Card; Daniel & Susan Cohen; Robert Cormier; Lois Ehlert; Jean Fritz; Gail E. Haley; James Howe; Brian Jacques; Paul Janeczko; Ursula K. Le Guin; Walter Dean Myers; Gary Paulsen; Bonnie Pryor; William Sleator; John Steptoe; David Wiesner; and Jane Yolen. Plus articles about school author visits, birth dates of authors and illustrators, and clip art. 3-ring binder. 109 pages. ISBN 0-938865-12-9. $26.95. April 1992.

School Library Management, 2nd edition by Anitra Gordon and Renee Naughton. This fact-filled resource provides a thorough coverage of school library management. Sections cover Goals & Objectives; Evaluation; Public Relations; Selection; Circulation; Processing; Weeding & Inventory; Clerks, Student Aides, & Volunteers; Budgeting; Computers & Technology; Organization; Discipline; Overdues; Forms; and Bibliography. 3-ring binder. 442 pages. ISBN 0-938865-06-4. $39.95. September 1991.

PR Notebook for School Librarians edited by Robert Graef and Renee Naughton. An in-depth look into every aspect of public relations in the school library. Topics covered are: Administration; Audiovisuals; Bulletin Boards; Events & Contests; Parents & the Community; Planning; Resources; Students; What PR Is; and Written Communications. 3-ring binder. 244 pages. ISBN 0-938865-01-3. $38.95. November 1990.

PGS Special Reports

Available Now! **Censorship: The Problem That Won't Go Away** by Edna M. Boardman. As a practicing school librarian, Edna Boardman has faced censorship challenges; here is her response to the censorship issue. Sections cover: Parents and the Library; Administrators and the Library; Dealing with Complaints; Professionalism; and Forms, Statements, and Policies. Includes bibliography. 80 pages. ISBN 0-938865-18-8. $16.95. March 1993.

New! **Creative Partnerships: Librarians and Teachers Working Together** by Lesley S. J. Farmer. This special report provides a wide range of ideas to promote and implement library service through cooperation with classroom teachers. Sections are: The Planning Process; Information Literacy; Programs & Services; Collection Development; Fund Raising; and Evaluation. Softcover. 75 pages. ISBN 0-938865-13-7. $16.95. January 1993.

Growing on the Job: Professional Development for the School Librarian by Edna M. Boardman. Whether you're just beginning or have been managing a school library for years, use this special report to develop your own professional growth plan. Sections are Defining Ourselves; After the Basics, What?; Growing Day-by-Day; Professional Ethics; Selected Readings; and Resources. Contains specific ideas for learning and growing in your profession. Softcover. 81 pages. ISBN 0-938865-10-2. $16.95. October 1991.

The BOOK REPORT & LIBRARY TALK Directory of Sources by Renee Naughton. A school library media specialist's one-stop source of information about suppliers and products. Among the resources: Audiovisual Supplies; Computer Software & Sources; Curriculum-Related Sources; Library Skills; Library Supply Companies; Magazine Agencies; Magazines For Students' Writings; Newsletters; Professional Journals; Public Relations Promotional Materials; Storytelling; and Booktalk Aids. Softcover. 105 pages. ISBN 0-938865-09-9. $19.95. October 1991.

THE BOOK REPORT Binder (#153) and **LIBRARY TALK Binder** (#161). Binders for your favorite magazines! Each binder will hold 2 volumes (10 issues) of THE BOOK REPORT or LIBRARY TALK. Each has an attractive design on the front cover and spine. As an extra plus, 4 sheets of clip art for school library promotion are included! Binders are $9.95 each. March 1992.

PGS Reprint Series
These books contain the best articles and tips from THE BOOK REPORT and LIBRARY TALK.

Now Available from Linworth! **Tips and Other Bright Ideas for School Librarians.** From THE BOOK REPORT's most popular column come 1200 bright ideas to assist in better managing your school library media center. These easy-to-implement ideas are field-tested and sure to work in your school library media center. Softcover. 125 pages. ISBN 0-87436-605-4. $24.95.

New! **Reading Motivation**, 2nd edition. Now in its second edition, this beneficial workbook will help you get the books off the shelves and into students' hands. Softcover. 110+ pages. ISBN 0-938865-26-9. $19.95. March 1993.

Library Research Skills Workbook: Grades 7-12. This informative workbook shares hundreds of ideas, exercises, and lessons reprinted from THE BOOK REPORT and written by junior and senior high school librarians. Softcover. 138 pages. ISBN 0-938865-00-5. $19.95. September 1990.

Curriculum Workbook. This handy workbook has practical, tested ideas for all aspects of curriculum planning. Spiral Bound. 116 pages. ISBN 0-938865-02-1. $19.95. November 1990.

ORDER FORM
THE BOOK REPORT and LIBRARY TALK

I would like to subscribe to THE BOOK REPORT: The Journal for Jr and Sr High School Librarians for: Amount
___1 year - $39.00   ___2 years - $70.00   ___3 years - $102.00   _____
I would like to subscribe to LIBRARY TALK: The Magazine for Elementary School Librarians for:
___1 year - $39.00   ___2 years - $70.00   ___3 years - $102.00   _____
I WOULD LIKE BOTH THE BOOK REPORT and LIBRARY TALK:
___SAVE! Special 1 year subscription rate of $70.00 for both. (Orders must be shipped to the same address.)   _____
Canadian Subscriptions - Add $8.00 per year per magazine

THE PROFESSIONAL GROWTH SERIES

Qty. Item	Price	Amount	Qty. Item	Price	Amount
___ 226 Multicultural Picture Books	$28.95	_____	___ 005 Library Research Skills Gr 7-12	$19.95	_____
___ 196 Skills for Life: Grades K-6	$34.95	_____	___ 021 Curriculum	$19.95	_____
___ 20X Skills for Life: Grades 6-8	$34.95	_____	___ 17X Instant Art Notebook	$34.95	_____
___ 218 Skills for Life: Grades 9-12	$34.95	_____	___ 285 Instant Art VI	$10.95	_____
___ 234 Looking Great with Video	$34.95	_____	___ 869 Instant Art V	$10.95	_____
___ 242 Winning Friends for the Library	$28.95	_____	___ 862 Instant Art IV	$10.95	_____
___ 056 Elem. School Librarian's Desk Ref.	$38.95	_____	___ 854 Instant Art III	$10.95	_____
___ 072 Making It With Media	$34.95	_____	___ 848 Instant Art II	$10.95	_____
___ 110 Lessons for the Library Student Staff	$29.95	_____			
___ 129 Author Profile Collection	$26.95	_____	Subtotal (both columns)............................. _____		
___ 064 School Library Management 2nd ed	$39.95	_____	Shipping & handling on Professional Growth Series		
___ 013 Public Relations for School Librarians	$38.95	_____	products only— in the U.S. add 9% with minimum charge		
___ 188 Censorship	$16.95	_____	of $4.25. FREE SHIPPING & HANDLING FOR		
___ 137 Creative Partnerships	$16.95	_____	PREPAID ORDERS! .... _____		
___ 102 Growing on the Job	$16.95	_____	All orders outside the U.S. pay actual postage.		
___ 099 Directory of Sources	$19.95	_____			
___ 153 The Book Report Binder	$ 9.95	_____	TOTAL AMOUNT DUE......................... $_____		
___ 161 Library Talk Binder	$ 9.95	_____	Prices subject to change.		
___ 054 Tips and Other Bright Ideas	$24.95	_____	All orders payable in U.S. funds only.		
___ 269 Reading Motivation 2nd ed	$19.95	_____	We guarantee delivery within 30 days! Thank you for your order!		

Satisfaction guaranteed with all of our products.
Your telephone number is requested in case we have questions concerning your
order (_____) _____-_____

SHIP TO: **BILL TO:**
                                                     Purchase Order # _____

_____ _____   _____ _____
Name   Title   Attention   Title

_____   _____
District/ School Name   District/ School Name

_____   _____
Address   Address

_____ _____ _____   _____ _____ _____
City   State   Zip+4   City   State   Zip+4

Please check the proper box(es) below: ☐ MasterCard   ☐ VISA
☐ Payment enclosed - Checks payable to: **Linworth Publishing, Inc.**   _ _ _ _ — _ _ _ _ — _ _ _ _ — _ _ _ _ ___ /___
☐ Purchase Order   480 E. Wilson Bridge Rd, Suite L   Charge Card Account #   Exp. Date
☐ Send invoice   Worthington, Ohio 43085-2372
☐ MasterCard/ VISA   (614) 436-7107, FAX (614) 436-9490   Signature
                                         (800) 786-5017